"This book is a must-read for any true student of history. Excellent reading for Americans, but also for anyone interested in how we have arrived in the modern world and where we may go from here."

> Steven G. Hall, PhD, associate professor
> Louisiana State University
> Member Au Sable Institute

"A much needed book for all who want to understand better the influence and impact of Christianity on history."

> Dr. Charles N. Neder, president
> Youth Conference Ministries, Chattanooga

"It's outrageous that history has been altered and few know that all the wonderful blessings we have in life come from Jesus Christ. Forgotten Foundation *is an incredible book."*

> Matt Bennett, founder and president of the Christian Union
> "Advancing the Kingdom of Christ in the Ivy League"

"Ideas drive culture. Our culture has forgotten how deeply Christianity has influenced and shaped basic values we hold dear in America. Russ Stevenson does an excellent job of reminding us of this strong connection."

> Elizabeth Green, former Campus Crusade for Christ
> staff member at Cornell and Dartmouth Universities

"At a time when the 'Western' world is doubting its religious heritage and rejecting its cultural values this book comes as a much needed reaffirmation of the Biblical beliefs and values on which Western civilization was built. In the world at large where its brightest young scholars look to Western educational institutions for scientific and cultural truth and guidance, this book brings light."

> Ned Hale, campus ministry staff
> With InterVarsity Christian Fellowship-USA, 1962-2006

"Russ Stevenson's Forgotten Foundation: How the Great Ideas of the Christian Faith Became the Foundation of the Western World *assists Christians in reminding those with an atheist worldview of the irreplaceable influence and receptivity of Christianity to an open, free search for truth."*

Katherine Shaw Spaht
Jules F. and Francis L. Landry Professor of Law
Louisiana State University

"Forgotten Foundation *addresses many of the hot button issues of the liberal left – science, academia, abolition of slavery, women's rights, democracy and moral values – and puts forth a clear and convincing argument that explains how Christianity played a central role in each. I highly recommend this book."*

Tony Perkins, president
Family Research Council
Washington, D.C.

"Taking up widely believed secularist revisions of Western history in order to remedy the resulting ignorance about the place of the Christian religion in our National life, Stevenson calls us to remember who we are and not to be fooled out of our title deeds. Forgotten Foundation *presents its wisdom in a thoroughly clear and useful form, down to the inclusion of study aids for church and other groups."*

Edward Hugh Henderson
Seynaeve Professor of Christian Studies
and Professor of Philosophy
Louisiana State University, Baton Rouge.

FORGOTTEN FOUNDATION

How the Great Ideas of the Christian Faith
Became the Foundation of the Western World

BY RUSS STEVENSON

*Forgotten Foundation: How the Great Ideas of the
Christian Faith Became the Foundation of the Western World*

Reformation Press
P.O. Box 2210
136 Tremont Park Drive
Lenoir, North Carolina 28645

Reformation Press books, monographs and other resources are available at special discounts in bulk purchases for educational and ministry use. For more details, contact:

Manager of Publications
Reformation Press
P.O. Box 2210
136 Tremont Park Drive
Lenoir, North Carolina 28645

Call us at 1-800-368-0110
Or visit Reformation Press on the Web at www.resourcecatalog.org

Cover Design: Sarah Golliher, www.golliherdesign.com, daughter of Russ Stevenson.

Printed in the United States of America

To my wife
Sherrill
my encourager

TABLE OF CONTENTS

ACKNOWLEDGEMENTS

The original idea for this book came from my experiences teaching "College Briefing Course" classes to scores of graduating high school seniors at First Presbyterian Church in Baton Rouge, Louisiana, and to an additional group of students, already in college, who regularly joined in the journey of those courses. One student, Rachel Hebert, even wrote a song including a reference to opalescent jellyfish, which I had used in an illustration. Another, Sarah Lunceford, wrote me a note that helped convince me that the course's great ideas should be gathered together in a book for broader dissemination.

I wrote the first draft during a winter sabbatical on the shores of Lake Champlain. Bob and Cookie Davenport met the needs of my wife and me with a snowplowed road, desserts, chicken soup, regular fuel deliveries, and a steady stream of the must-read books I ordered through Cookie.

Along the way, the encouragement of all those with whom I have shared the book's concept has been invaluable. Their suggestions began before I even started writing and served as a great GPS as I found my way through the journey of this book.

The writings of Rodney Stark, former professor of sociology and comparative religion at the University of Washington, were the primary catalyst for this book, conceptually, specifically *One True God* and *For the Glory of God*, published by the Princeton University Press. To Dr. Stark I give my deepest thanks.

When the first draft was done, several people agreed to take a copy and give me their comments and suggested revisions. This was an invaluable step in the process. I thank Dr. Steven Hall, professor at Louisiana State University; Garnett Slatton, pastor of River Community Church in

Prairieville, La.; Dr. Philip I. Woerner and his wife Barbara in Springfield, Ill.; Nancy Johnson, lifelong friend and fellow camper at Lake Champlain; Dr. Bucky Hunsicker, pastor at Stuart Presbyterian Church in Stuart, Va., and his wife Matilda; our four daughters (and their spouses): Elizabeth and Howard Green, Joanna and John Woodworth, Sarah and Sean Golliher and Mary and Derek Anderson; Sue Miley, a River Community Church member; and, most of all, Lloyd Lunceford, who put in countless hours editing, making suggestions and even offering ideas for additional material.

Finally, my wife Sherrill has typed more drafts of this manuscript than could ever be counted. Her work – and her constant encouragement along the way – have been invaluable.

Russ Stevenson
Gonzales, Louisiana

FORGOTTEN FOUNDATION

*How the Great Ideas of the Christian Faith
Became the Foundation of the Western World*

INTRODUCTION

As a college student, my mind was compartmentalized. In my classes, I was learning about the world around me and gaining a liberal arts education that was among the best available. I was also learning about God and the Bible as an active member of several college Christian groups, which, I later discovered, were among the most vital in the country. But I had a hard time putting the two "learnings" together, the Christian perspective and the liberal arts perspective. I remember longing to hear sermons that would help me integrate the two worlds, sermons that had to do with "real life." The secular university I attended had no interest in making a connection between Christian faith and collegiate subjects. At least one of the Christian groups addressed the integration-of-knowledge problem by telling us there were certain courses at the university – especially in the religion department – that were so destructive of faith that a Christian simply should not take them.

As a direct result, I lost my faith the summer after graduation. I felt forced to choose between two worlds: the legitimacy and importance of what I had learned in college on the one hand and the Christian faith on the other. The points at which these two perspectives ground against each other became points of doubt. That summer, I decided to resolve these differences and work through my doubts. The doubts won. I decided I could no longer be a Christian and entered a brief period of atheism. Ironically, I later went to seminary to test this lifetime decision and slowly returned to the Christian faith. But that is another story.

Today's students often face a similar experience. The Higher Education Research Institute at the University of California-Los Angeles released a recent study of religions and spiritual attitudes among college students.

They found that the evangelical revival, which has impacted all of America in recent years, had touched college students as well. Christian groups are strong; three out of four students say they pray; one in five is "highly religious." In contrast to the libertine students of the 1960s, there is a rise in the number of students who say they are virgins. But today's secularized college education does little to help students in their religious and moral quests. Although three out of four students in the UCLA poll said they were "searching for meaning and purpose in life," more than half said those questions are ignored in their classes.[1]

My own college experience led me to cherish any book that helps me with the integration of Christian and secular knowledge. Over the years, these books have become my favorites, and I have found myself returning to them again and again. At the outset, I want to acknowledge my debt to their authors and publishers. The first was a book by Glen Tinder titled *The Political Meaning of Christianity* and published by Louisiana State University Press. Then came Michael Denton's *Evolution: A Theory in Crisis* and *The Soul of Science* by Nancy Pearcey and Charles Thaxton. After that, *Personal Knowledge* by Michael Polanyi and *The Question of God* by Armand Nicholi Jr., made an indelible impression. Finally, two books by Rodney Stark, mentioned above, provided the immediate impetus for this book.

This is a book about "great ideas" and will argue that the great ideas that have shaped American life and Western civilization find their source in the Christian faith. Ideas have consequences. And great ideas change the world, for good or ill. As journalist George F. Will put it in a recent speech,

> A long life in journalism and around Washington, D.C., has
> taught me not just that ideas have consequences, but that only
> ideas have large and lasting consequences.[2]

Not everyone affected by a great idea knows what the idea is, but, nevertheless, such ideas change history and shape cultures. Karl Marx had the idea that, "from each according to his ability; to each according to his need." It didn't work. But 60 million Russians died in its aftermath – 60 years of a kind of national slavery. Adolf Hitler had the idea of a master race, built on the Darwinian idea of survival of the fittest and the Nietzschean idea that power matters more than morality. World War II was the result. But many men who fought the war – on both sides – really had little, if any, understanding that, at least in part, they were combatants in an ivory-tower war started by Darwin and Nietzsche.

As I write this, Iran has an idea it calls "the China model" – a Muslim oligarchy (original idea: Muhammad) combined with a capitalist economy (original idea: Adam Smith). Just next door, the people of Iraq and Afghanistan turned out for democratic elections in astonishing numbers. They have been influenced by what is being called "the Bush Doctrine" – the idea that it is the natural, God-given yearning of the human heart to be free. In Lebanon, Palestine, Egypt and Saudi Arabia, sympathetic notes of the same tune have played spontaneously. The United States was founded on the Christian idea that men are "endowed by their Creator with certain unalienable rights, that among these are life, liberty, and the pursuit of happiness."[3] That idea in the Declaration of Independence has had a profound effect on the history of this nation – even for people who cannot quote it or are entirely unaware of it.

Years ago, I visited South America for a summer and discovered that democracy wasn't working very well anywhere on that continent. The reason was apparent to even a casual observer: Nobody had a truly democratic mindset. The standard, deeply ingrained ideal of leadership was that of the *caudillo* – the charismatic, benign leader who, for all practical purposes, functions as a dictator. South Americans were trying democracy, yet a different idea was still shaping political life. I was just a college student there for the summer, but the problem was obvious to me.

The people who shape the world are the people who shape our ideas. We may not know their names. We may not even be aware of the ideas themselves – or why the ideas are different ("Doesn't everybody think this way?"). But they shape the way we think. The movers and shakers of the world have never been the generals or the politicians – the movers and shakers are the idea makers, the thinkers. Sometimes their ideas have horrible and destructive consequences. And sometimes their ideas are great, truly wonderful, a profound blessing.

Where did modern civilization come from? I propose that modern civilization sprang from a handful of great ideas, which find their origin in the Christian faith. Because this fact is so little understood, these ideas – indeed, the essential pillars of modern civilization – are invisible to most people. Modern man has no sense of how influential the Christian faith has been to the formation of the civilization we enjoy today. This influence was first felt in the West but, in the last few centuries, its influence has stretched across the globe. It is the forgotten foundation.

I've called these ideas "great" because they are big. They reach to the depth of the nature and meaning of life. They are what long ago philosophers called "metaphysics" – i.e., beyond physics. They have to do with whether there is a God – and, if so, how the world is related to the God who created it – why we are here and how we should live.

Very big ideas are directly connected to personal worldviews. The first chapter, therefore, is a consideration of worldviews – what some people call "religions." In ordinary conversation, we don't talk about worldviews ("religion and politics") because they tend to be conversation stoppers. But they can't be avoided. For each of us, our worldview is ultimately the basis for how we think about life. If great ideas make up the superstructure on which a culture is built, then that superstructure is built upon the worldview of that culture. Great ideas originate from and are a byproduct of particular worldviews. So any discussion of a "cluster" of great ideas must begin with an examination of the worldview from which they flow.

Chapters two through seven examine six "great ideas," which, together, form the foundation of modern civilization. These ideas were crucial to the rise of science (chapter two), our understanding of knowledge (chapter three), the abolition of slavery (chapter four), the equality of men and women (chapter five), the shape of democracy (chapter six), and the morality that makes commerce, the family and humane life, in general, thrive (chapter seven). All of them, I will attempt to show, come from the Christian faith. Without them, those who live in the West would have a significantly different cultural experience, perhaps even chaos and anarchy. There is, in other words, an historic truth about how this world of human interaction and progress we call "civilization" came into being that has been neglected. This book explores that truth.

Chapter Eight addresses well-known historical events that are used regularly to accuse the Christian faith of having been a detrimental influence on the development of civilization. And, finally, chapter nine examines the implications of these "great ideas" for the truth of the Christian faith.

So, to begin at the beginning, let's start with a look at worldviews in general and, specifically, the Christian worldview from which the great ideas we'll be looking at originate.

CHAPTER ONE

WORLDVIEWS

E veryone has a worldview. Quite simply, a worldview is an individual's understanding of what life is all about. It is the set of lenses that colors what one sees; it is a person's assumptions about the nature and meaning of life. Worldviews are the big ideas that shape individual lives.

Toward the end of his life, influenced by the Romantic Movement, the artist Paul Gauguin moved to Tahiti, where he expected to find the joys of a primitive life of innocence – as Romanticism promised. Instead, he experienced a lack of acceptance by the native population, found himself in poverty (often eating the contents of a tin can right out of the can), and contracted syphilis. Shortly before his death, he painted his most famous painting as an expression of his disillusionment with Romanticism and his consequent loss of meaning and direction. He titled it, "Who Are We? Where Did We Come From? Where Are We Going?"

Those three questions are basic worldview questions. Answer those for yourself and you have described the biggest piece of your worldview.

EVERYONE HAS A WORLDVIEW

In his book, *Why Religion Matters*, Huston Smith says that wherever or whenever people live, they always face three inescapable problems: How to obtain food and shelter, how to get along with others and how to relate themselves to "the total scheme of things."[1] A person's worldview is his set of assumptions about the total scheme of things, "what life is all about." Smith, an internationally known author on the subject of world religions, says worldviews are like peripheral vision. They provide the "background" we assume for all our experiences of life. [2] They provide the overall picture that helps us make sense of what happens to us – and also to make decisions about the future. But the really important thing, he says, is this:

> The deeper fact, however, is that to have or not have a worldview
> is not an option, for peripheral vision always conditions what
> we are attending to focally. ... The only choice we have is to be
> consciously aware of our worldviews and criticize them where
> they need criticizing, or to let them work on us unnoticed and to
> acquiesce to living unexamined lives.[3]

Our worldview is our understanding of the lay of the land as we live life. It is the "big picture" through which we orient ourselves to life's trials and opportunities. Perhaps the most surprising thing about a worldview, according to Smith, is that though we all have one – our own set of operating assumptions about life – for many, even most, those assumptions are "unexamined," unarticulated. If asked, "So, what is your worldview?" many would give a worrisome answer: "Well, I really don't know."

Even more surprising is the fact that people who think they know what their worldview is actually may have no clue at all. This may explain why polls indicate such a high percentage of Americans "believe in God" when, in actuality, they have nothing to do with God at all. It's just theoretical. It's just the assumed right answer. God is not a part of their big picture of life in any significant way.

People are often very inconsistent about their worldviews. In his book, *Habits of the Heart*, Robert Bellah, the famous sociologist at the University of California-Berkeley, writes of a woman named Sheila who coined the word "Sheilaism"[4] to describe her own beliefs. A "Sheilaism" has come to mean any personal belief invented or selected by an individual. Thus, a religion of "Sheilaisms" is a made-up, hodgepodge religion – as, for example, would be the case with someone who believes in God and in the Bible as God's Word, does not believe Jesus is the Son of God, yet does believe in reincarnation.

People sometimes see religions – and to that extent, worldviews – as a smorgasbord. You take what you like and skip what you don't. One's authority for that choice is simply, "Well, that's what I think." People just make it up as they go along. They make up their own worldview, their own God, out of whole cloth.

This process is just ancient idolatry in modern garb. The Prophet Isaiah described it like this:

> The carpenter ... cuts down cedars, or perhaps a cypress or oak.
> ... Half of the wood he burns in the fire; over it he prepares his
> meal, he roasts his meat and eats his fill. He also warms himself
> and says, "Ah! I am warm; I see the fire." From the rest he makes
> a god, his idol; he bows down to it and worships. He prays to it
> and says, "Save me; you are my god." They know nothing, they
> understand nothing; their eyes are plastered over so they cannot
> see, and their minds closed so they cannot understand. No one
> stops to think, no one has the knowledge or understanding to say,
> "Half of it I used for fuel; I even baked bread over its coals, I
> roasted meat and I ate. Shall I make a detestable thing from what
> is left? Shall I bow down to a block of wood?"[5]

An example of this unthinking inconsistency is found in people who live as if there is no God but call themselves agnostics. To call oneself an agnostic is to say, "I don't know if there is a God. It's not my fault. I just don't have enough information." To call oneself an atheist, however, is to make a decision – it is to say, "I believe there is no God." In truth, most people who call themselves agnostics live as atheists. God is just not a part of their big picture, their worldview.

If we exclude all the Sheilaisms, all the I-made-it-up-myself worldviews, there are only a limited number of alternatives for the basic framework of a worldview:

1. There is one God (monotheism).
2. There are many gods (polytheism).
3. There is no God (atheism).
4. There is only God (pantheism).

Postmodernism is sometimes offered as a fifth alternative: "Whatever!" or "There are no metanarratives." But postmodernism is really just another form of the operating assumption of atheism. As Philip J. Sampson puts it in his book, *Six Modern Myths about Christianity and Western Civilization*, "[P]ostmodern stories are skeptical of whether any all-embracing truth exists."[6] Postmodernism is a reaction against the modern reliance upon reason and truth. Instead, it turns to stories, skeptical of whether those stories will or should fit together in a greater whole or lead to the discovery of a one-and-only truth.

In this regard, postmodernism and existentialism are cut from the same cloth. Existentialism, with its emphasis on finding meaning in the present, is also generally skeptical of the importance of any overarching truth.

Today's pantheistic alternatives are rooted in Eastern religions, which tend to express the best insights of man on the subject of the riddle of life and how to live it. They make little or no claim, however, to be "revelation." They are essentially here-and-now coping religions, which attempt to give wise and true answers to the question of how to achieve happiness in life. Some of them, like Taoism and Confucianism, are essentially codes of ethics that attempt no answer to the ultimate question, "Is there a God?"

Nevertheless, pantheism has become hugely influential in the modern world. From *Star Wars* ("The Force is with you.") and the phrase, "the divine spark in all living things," to much of today's environmental philosophy, pantheism seems to be everywhere. But pantheism tends to be amoral in the sense that the distinction between good and evil loses meaning. If all is God and God is one, then all is one whether good or evil, health or sickness, Creator or creature. Distinctions fade. Differences are an illusion.[7] As one reflects on this, it becomes apparent that the actual practice of pantheism in the real world is, for all intents and purposes, impossible. Yet the cultural influence of pantheism is broad, though unrecognized by the many who repeat its mantras.

TWO BASIC ALTERNATIVE WORLDVIEWS

In the world of Western thought, no one is going to be a traditional polytheist, but pantheistic Taoism, Confucianism and Buddhism tend to degrade to polytheism in their popular forms.[8] So, in the general world of ideas today there are really only two alternatives for the basic framework of a worldview: monotheism and atheism. And, for reasons that will become clear as this book proceeds, those two alternatives tend to boil down to Christianity (monotheism) and scientific reductionism (atheism).

To say just a word about this, there are really only three monotheisms: Judaism, Islam and Christianity – all related and, therefore, often referred to as the three "Abrahamic faiths." Because Judaism has become an ethnic, or heritage-related, religion (rather than the one truth to be proclaimed to the world) and because Islam is so culturally foreign to the modern mind,[9] Christianity emerges as the only currently viable monotheistic answer to the question of the real truth about our existence, the true worldview.

Scientific reductionism (alternately called scientism, naturalism or materialism) is the other alternative. It is the belief that everything "reduces" to matter, that life and human consciousness and concerns about morals and meaning have all arisen in a universe whose basic building block is a lifeless atom. It is the belief that, in the famous words of Carl Sagan, author of the PBS television series *Cosmos*, "The cosmos is all there is or ever was or ever will be." No God, no meaning, no purpose – just matter. Values and morality are arrived at by reason alone and have no transcendent source or authority. In this worldview, the scientific method is the only means of finding truth. As Huston Smith summarizes it,

> For the knowledge class in our industrialized Western civilization, it has come to seem self-evident that the scientific account of the world gives us its full story and that the supposed transcendent realities of which religions speak are at best doubtful.[10]

In his book, *The Mysterious Flame*, Colin McGinn dramatizes the view of man that scientism proposes. In an exchange between an alien explorer just returned from an Earth visit, and his commander, the explorer describes what human beings are:

Explorer: "They're made out of meat."

Commander: "Meat?"

Explorer: "There's no doubt about it. We picked several from different parts of the planet, took them aboard our recon vessels, and probed them all the way through. They're completely meat."

Commander: "That's impossible. What about the radio signals? The messages to the stars?"

Explorer: "They made the machines. That's what I'm trying to tell you. Meat made the machines."

Commander: "That's ridiculous. How can meat make a machine? You're asking me to believe in sentient meat?"

Explorer: "I'm not asking you; I'm telling you. These creatures are the only sentient race in the sector and they're made out of meat."

Commander: "Maybe they're like the Orfolei. You know, a carbon-based intelligence that goes through a meat stage."

Explorer: "Nope. They're born meat and they die meat. We studied them for several of their life-spans, which didn't take too long. Do you have any idea of the life-span of meat?"

Commander: "Spare me. Okay, maybe they're only part meat. You know, like the Weddilei. A meat head with an electron plasma brain inside."

Explorer: "Nope. We thought of that since they do have meat heads like the Weddilei. But I told you, we probed them. They're meat all the way through."

Commander: "No brain?"

Explorer: "Oh, there's a brain all right. It's just that the brain is made of meat."

Commander: "So ... what does the thinking?"

Explorer: "You're not understanding, are you? The brain does the thinking. The meat."

Commander: "Thinking meat! You are asking me to believe in thinking meat!"

Explorer: "Yes, thinking meat. Conscious meat! Loving meat! Dreaming meat! The meat is the whole deal."[11]

Scientific reductionism postulates that "meat" is all there is to human beings. Christianity claims that, though we are made of dust, we are beings made in the image of God. These two worldviews see things very differently.

That difference is characterized by Richard Dawkins in a recent book titled *A Devil's Chaplain: Reflections on Hope, Lies, Science and Love.* Dawkins is the Charles Simonyi Professor of the Public Understanding of Science at Oxford University. Dawkins' final chapter, "Good and Bad Reasons for Believing," contains a letter to his ten-year-old daughter, Juliet, in which he asks and answers the question, "How do we know something is true?"[12] There is only one good reason for believing something is true, he says, and that is "evidence." He contrasts this with three bad reasons: "tradition, authority and revelation."

By "evidence," he does not necessarily mean scientific evidence, as is true of his example of the evidence behind the sentence, "My wife loves me." But he does quite clearly say that, in his opinion, when it comes to religion, all religion is based, not on evidence, but on "tradition, authority and revelation." What he fails to understand is that all religions involve evidence as well as faith. Just as important, he fails to understand that his own worldview is not based solely on evidence, but also requires faith. How does he know there is no God? He doesn't. He takes a leap of faith from the "evidence" to that conclusion.

His worldview is atheistic. Christianity's is theistic. Both involve evidence. Both involve faith. Neither can be proven. Dawkins' claim that Christianity is not based on evidence at all, though, is both ignorant and foolhardy. Many people happen to believe that the evidence for the existence of a good Creator God is far greater than the evidence for atheism. Dawkins has a worldview, a basic understanding of what life is all about. He fails to realize that to say that matter is all there is is ultimately a faith statement – as all worldviews are.

WORLDVIEWS SHAPE HOW WE SEE LIFE

Your worldview makes all the difference in how you see life. Those who believe that nature is all there is – and, specifically, nature that has evolved through the survival of the fittest and the extinction of the weak – face a dark abyss. Making our own meaning in a meaningless universe, building our lives on love in a universe whose only building blocks are lifeless atoms, is a daunting task. To the ancient question, "Is the universe friendly?" the answer of scientific reductionism is "No" – and that is a real downer.

Many parents face the issue of worldviews when raising children. Recently, my eye caught an article titled, "Blind Faith: Is there a God? And which matters more – what I believe or what I want my boys to believe?" Written by a young woman with two boys in the two- to three-year-old range, the article described her beliefs very tentatively: "Well, I'd say I'm agnostic. I think it's impossible to know whether or not God exists. It's not that I definitely don't believe, but ... I'm skeptical."

She especially faces this issue at Christmastime, the celebration of Jesus' birth. Is this a celebration of a real event, the birth of the real Savior, sent by a real God, or is it just a fairy tale? How should she raise her boys? "What will I say when Henry turns to me and says, 'What happens when you die?' or 'Is there a God?'" she asks. "Life is easier with faith ... particularly for children, to believe that things happen for a reason, that there is an order, a Divine hand guiding us through our days. To raise a child with no religion means a tacit acceptance of the idea that what happens in this world is random, that chaos is the rule not the exception."[13]

She is right. These are the choices today: scientific reductionism on the one hand, Christian faith on the other. She is wrong, of course, in characterizing faith in God as "blind." There are ways of knowing other than the scientific method. At the practical level of our lives, we accept and use these ways of knowing every day. She does not know her husband loves her on the basis of the scientific method. It's just a different kind of knowing. The Christian faith is not "blind." It's based on a great deal of evidence that makes faith reasonable – the evidence of nature, history and experience. Science is not the only way of "knowing."

A life based on the faith statement, "There is no God," is a life that sees human consciousness as an anomaly in an unconscious world, as "just the meat talking." The universe is not friendly. It is dead – just lifeless atoms, nothing more. There is no meaning, no reason for optimism, no meaningful love, no free will.

Albert Camus characterized living in a world without meaning or God as being like the Greek myth of Sisyphus. Sisyphus was condemned to the pointless task of rolling a huge rock up a hill, only to have to repeat his effort in an endless cycle when the rock inevitably rolled back down. Eventually, Camus came to believe that the existentialism he had espoused was a dead end. Toward the end of his life, Camus sought to be baptized as a Christian, reaching out to find a source of light and hope in a world of meaninglessness, darkness and despair.[14]

Recently, I had a discussion with an old college friend. He had retired after a successful professional life. Since retirement, he had been actively volunteering his time in the community, but he was nearing the end of his life and was discouraged. Life seemed bleak and without meaning. He had been unable to believe in "virgin births, resurrections and all that stuff." He had lived his life without God but would probably call himself an agnostic rather than an atheist. Since worldviews shape how we see life, I suggested that he reconsider the Christian faith. I told him life does not have to end in despair. It can end in hope and confidence in God.

THE CHRISTIAN WORLDVIEW

The starting point of the Christian worldview is the conviction that life is good because the God who created everything (including life) is good. It is grounded in the conviction that "God is light and in Him is no darkness at all"[15] and that "God is love."[16] Christians believe it is neither foolish nor ignorant to believe that "faith, hope, love abide, these three. But the greatest of these is love."[17] The whole Bible, in fact, is God's love story.

In the midst of all the tragedy, evil and suffering in this world, Christians believe that those things are not the whole story. We believe that, in the end, good wins because God is good and God is God.

But this is not at the expense of realism. The Christian faith also sees this life as a great battle between good and evil and the great need of the world as salvation from evil and its result, death and separation from God.

Most surprisingly, the Christian faith solves the problem of a good Creator and a world infected by evil by God Himself coming into the world He made. In the person of Jesus Christ, God came to suffer and die and rise from death to "redeem" the world from sin and death. This is what the New Testament calls "grace;" God in His love doing for us what we could not do for ourselves. Our part is to simply respond. We reach out, let God love us, surrender to Him and place our faith in Jesus Christ. He then becomes not just *the* Savior but *our* Savior.

So, the Christian worldview is that we are not alone. We have been created by a God of love. He has made us in His image and, therefore, we are capable of fellowship with Him. He promises to shepherd us through our lives and take us to be with Him when we die. He transforms our lives here and now as well, and makes us partners on Earth in the great work of His Kingdom.

There is a radical realism here: We all have turned away from God. There is radical joy here: God loves us and suffered for us so that by simply accepting His love and forgiveness, we might become His forever children. There is radical value here: We are all created in God's image and called into His family by faith. There is radical work here: God gives our lives eternal meaning by giving us eternal work to do. There is radical optimism here: We know how it all turns out – Jesus wins!

The outlook of the Christian faith is summed up in an ancient Christian hymn dating from at least the 7th century, and perhaps as early as the 5th, called "St. Patrick's Breastplate." It reads, in part:

> I arise today
> Through a mighty strength, the invocation of the Trinity,
> Through belief in the threeness,
> Through confession of the oneness
> Of the Creator of Creation... .

I arise today
Through the strength of heaven:
Light of sun,
Radiance of moon,
Splendor of fire,
Speed of lightning,
Swiftness of wind,
Depth of sea,
Stability of earth,
Firmness of rock.

I arise today
Through God's strength to pilot me;
God's might to uphold me,
God's wisdom to guide me,
God's eye to look before me,
God's ear to hear me,
God's Word to speak for me,
God's hand to guard me,
God's way to lie before me,
God's host to save me
From snares of devils,
From temptations of vices,
From everyone who shall wish me ill,
Afar and anear,
Alone and in multitude.[18]

THE CHRISTIAN WORLDVIEW AND AMERICA

The Christian worldview forms the background of American culture – the background of Western culture as a whole, in fact. It is the root of American optimism. At the same time, that influence has been tremendously overlooked – witness the fact that there is no reference to God in either the rejected constitution of the European Union or the Treaty of Lisbon, its proposed replacement.

There is a whole segment in today's society of well-educated people who have no sense of the enormous debt our culture owes to the Christian faith. Richard Dawkins, the Oxford professor, is just one of those people.

How can he hold the university position he does, yet be unaware of the fact that the Christian faith, as we shall see in the next chapter, gave birth to science?

A recent book by Sam Harris, a Stanford graduate completing his doctorate in neuroscience, is titled *The End of Faith: Religion, Terror and the Future of Reason*. Published in 2004, the book claims that all the troubles of the world have been caused by religion. As Harris puts it, "A glance at history ... reveals that ideas which divide one group of human beings from another, only to unite them in slaughter, generally have their roots in religion."[19]

He believes that because some religions have unhappy consequences, all religions are bad. His argument is akin to pointing out that some mothers abuse and even kill their children; therefore, the main problem with the family as an institution throughout the world is mothers. He has no sense that not everyone who claims to be a Christian is a Christian, as defined by Christian orthodoxy throughout the ages and by the Bible itself. He has no sense that Christians do not always act in Christian ways, no sense of the great gifts the Christian faith has given to the world and certainly no sense of his own cultural debt to the Christian faith.

By way of a careful selection of facts and a voluminous bibliography composed only of books by likeminded authors, he simply writes off all religion as believing "the truth of propositions for which no evidence is even conceivable."[20] He claims there is no God and we'd better get used to it.[21] He says that uncontaminated reason alone should be our guide, seeming utterly oblivious to the fact that the greatest murderers of the 20th century – Hitler, Stalin, Mao Tse-Tung and Pol Pot – were not religiously motivated at all. Stalin killed 60 million of his own subjects and Hitler killed six million Jews, not to mention all those on both sides of the Second World War who lost their lives, both citizens and soldiers.

It is no secret that Christianity, by and large, has no place at the table of ideas in America and the wider Western world. Television and radio commentator Sean Hannity, in his recent book, *Deliver Us From Evil*, feels he has to defend the concept of evil. "How," he asks, "could anyone witness the horrors of September 11th [2001], or the mass graves discovered in Iraq after the fall of Saddam Hussein, and dismiss the idea of evil?"[22] "To some," he says, "people like Saddam Hussein and Osama bin Laden are not morally depraved murderers, but men driven to their bad acts by the injustices of Western Society."[23] As journalist Ann Coulter has said, "To many of the elites today, Christianity just doesn't ring a bell. The religion that has transformed Western Civilization for two millennia is a blank slate for liberals."[24]

The fact is, many people do not realize they live in a society with Christian roots. In a recent coffee table book published by Princeton University, *Princeton University: The First 250 Years*, the author opens with the words, "At its start, Princeton, like other early American colleges, was a child of the church. But ..."[25] After the word, "but," the author does his best to distance the university from its Christian beginnings as fast and as far as possible. He talks of Princeton as a "feisty offspring" (of the church), "born of fierce controversy" when America was "wrestling with fundamental questions of identity." The clear implication being that this feisty offspring was rebellious and quickly turned away from its unfortunate narrow beginnings. The author has no sense of the depth of this country's Christian roots, nor of the role of Princeton in planting and nurturing them.

None of the author's implications, of course, is true. It is simply reflective of a modern embarrassment with the Christian faith. And that modern embarrassment leads not only to a disparagement of the role of the Christian faith in the shaping of our culture – but to a complete ignorance of it.

As a result, not everyone realizes the immense contributions of the Christian faith to the culture in which we live. This is true even of some otherwise well-informed folks. That ignorance leads to a neglect of Christianity and to an attitude of fear toward it. People tend to fear what they do not know or understand. Some people are terrified of Christians and their political influence. The argument can be made, however, that these "extremists" on the "Christian Right" are merely calling us back to the chief source of the historical blessings our culture enjoys.

In fact, the Christian faith is largely responsible for what is good in the civilization we enjoy today. The Christian desacralization of nature is the essential crucible out of which came modern science. It was the Christian understanding of the dignity of man, as created in the image of God, that was the root conviction in the worldwide abolition of slavery. Likewise, American democracy, the emancipation of women, the idea of the university and the moral perspective that says the family is the basic building block of society are all deeply rooted in the Christian beginnings of this country and the Christian foundation of Western civilization.

The great ideas of the world, good and bad, grow out of worldviews. This book is about some of the great ideas of the Christian worldview that have changed the West and the world.

Why is it that science did not begin in ancient Greece or India or Africa? Why is it that, until 150 years ago, slavery had been (or was being) practiced in every society that could afford it – and that the modern abolition of slavery began in Christian England? Why is it that human dignity – and, therefore, human rights – were so important in the founding of this country? These and other great ideas that produced Western civilization as we know it find their primary origin in the Christian faith. And, so, we turn to examining six key areas of Christian influence in the United States and in Western culture.

CHAPTER TWO

CHRISTIANITY AND THE
RISE OF SCIENCE

There's an old song by George Gershwin that says, "They all laughed at Christopher Columbus when he said the world was round." [1] But nothing could be further from the truth. The fact is, every educated person at the time of Columbus knew the world was round. The only controversy surrounding Columbus' 1492 voyage to the New World had to do with its length. Columbus thought it was about 2,800 miles to Japan, whereas it is actually about 14,000 miles, as the crow flies.

Jeffrey Burton Russell, a Middle Ages scholar, has said that during the first 15 centuries of the Christian faith – from the time of Christ to the time of Columbus – "nearly unanimous scholarly opinion pronounced the Earth spherical." [2] An engraving from a textbook on Ptolemy's cosmology, published by Poland's University of Krakow at about the time of Columbus, shows the sphere of the world with the "Arctic Pole," the "Antarctic Pole," the Equator and the Tropics of Capricorn and Cancer clearly marked. [3]

So why did all of us grow up thinking that at the time of that voyage to the New World everyone but Columbus, and especially church officials, thought the world was flat?

The answer is found in an 1896 book by the founder and first president of Cornell University, Andrew Dickson White (1832-1918). Titled *A*

History of the Warfare Between Science with Theology in Christendom, it claims,

> The warfare of Columbus [with religion] the world knows well:
> how the Bishop of Centa worsted him in Portugal; how sundry
> wise men of Spain confronted him with the usual quotations from
> Psalms, from St. Paul, and from St. Augustine; how, even after
> he was triumphant, and after his voyage had greatly strengthened
> the theory of the earth's sphericity ... the Church by its highest
> authority solemnly stumbled and persisted in going astray.[4]

It was all lies. White was simply grinding the axe of his own anti-Christian perspective, yet his book became hugely influential and has only been widely discredited in recent years. So, many educated people today believe there is a basic conflict between science and religion largely because of the influence of White's book – even though they may not have read it or even heard of it. The fact is that the culture in which they live, Western culture of the last 100 years, has, as a whole, been deeply influenced by one man's spurious claims against Christianity.

THE CRUCIBLE OF CHRISTENDOM

Science was birthed in the crucible of medieval European Christianity, coming out of the ideas and perspectives of the Christian faith. In fact, it was *only* in the Western Christian world that science arose. It did not arise out of the atheism or deism of the Renaissance, which appeared on the stage of history long after science began. It did not arise out of animism, the commonly held belief, 500 years ago, that spirit gods inhabited mountain, lakes and streams. It did not arise out of Japan's ancestor worship or Chinese Confucianism's moral teachings, though significant technology did. It did not arise out of India's Hinduism or Buddhism. It did not arise out of Islam, though significant advances in mathematics did. It arose only once in history, in Christian medieval Europe.[5] Why?

SCIENCE AND TECHNOLOGY

It is essential to make a distinction between science and technology. Science arose long after the Iron and Bronze Ages and the technological advancement of all sorts of metalworking. It arose after the discovery of gun powder and the advances in mathematics occasioned by Arabic numerals. The distinction is as follows:

Science is not merely technology. A society does not have science simply because it can build sailing ships, smelt iron, or eat off porcelain dishes. *Science* is a *method* utilized in *organized* efforts to formulate *explanations of nature*, always subject to modifications and corrections through *systematic observations*.

Put another way, science consists of two components: *theory* and *research*. Theorizing is the explanatory part of science. Scientific theories are *abstract statements* about *why* and *how* some portion of nature (including human social life) fits together and works. However, not all abstract statements, not even all of those offering explanations, qualify as scientific theories; otherwise, theology would be a science. Rather, abstract statements are scientific only if it is possible to deduce from them some definite predictions and prohibitions about what will be observed. And that's where research comes in.[6]

In a sense, technology is as old as man, but not science. Even the most primitive arrowheads and implements of the Stone Age are technology, but not science.

THE CONNECTION BETWEEN SCIENCE AND CHRISTIANITY

So what is it about Christianity that gave rise to science? It is a great idea of the Christian faith that *the world is comprehensible because it existed first in the mind and plan of God*. The world is not capricious; there is an order to things. As Albert Einstein famously said, "God doesn't play dice." And because the physical universe makes sense, it can be studied and understood. As Einstein again offered, "The eternal mystery of the world is its comprehensibility."[7]

The "mystery of comprehensibility" is the sense that, in studying the universe, one mind understands something another mind has "written."

In the Search for Extraterrestrial Intelligence (the SETI project), scientists look for signs of intelligent life elsewhere in the universe. With radio telescopes they look for incoming messages from beings somewhere out there who have minds as we do. Or they send spacecraft flying off beyond the solar system with messages designed to show intelligent beings somewhere out there that there is intelligent life here on earth. The search is a search of minds trying to make contact with other minds.

Einstein's point is that the comprehensibility of the universe is amazing because it is really one mind comprehending what another mind has done.

Science is like a search for extraterrestrial intelligence that hits the jackpot. The comprehensibility of the physical universe, in other words, points toward the mind and plan of the Creator Himself.

In the words of Genesis:

> In the beginning God created the heavens and the earth. ... God saw everything that He had made, and behold it was very good.[8]

And in the Psalms:

> The heavens are telling the glory of God; and the firmament proclaims His handiwork.[9]

The first scientists were Christians studying God's handiwork who, in so doing, believed they were interacting with the mind of God. They were thinking God's thoughts after Him. They commonly spoke of God's two books, both of which reveal His glory: the book of His Word, the Bible, and the book of His works, the universe and everything in it.

One of the effects of this perspective was that the Christian faith desacralized nature. One cannot very well study nature if it is inhabited by spirits who may take revenge if their territory is invaded. The Christian faith taught that nature was not inhabited, but created. To study it, therefore, was to study the ways, laws and artistry of the great Creator God. The assumption was that the world made sense because it existed first in the mind of God.

Finally, God gave man authority to "fill the earth and subdue it; and have dominion over ... every living thing that moves upon the earth"[10] and endowed man with Divine authority to "handle" nature, to shape it and to understand it. Genesis 2 tells us:

> The Lord God formed every beast of the field and every bird of the air and brought them to Adam to see what he would call them; and whatever the man called every living creature, that was its name.[11]

In ancient times, to name was to have authority over. It was far more than deciding to call one's pet cow "Bertha." It was to have the right to domesticate Bertha, to milk her and to put a fence around her. It was to assert dominance over Bertha and her destiny.

All of this meant that the act of observation and experimentation within nature became a God-given right of human beings – the right to practice science.

The desacralization of nature made the practice of science safe, the gift of dominion made it justified and the link to theology made it attractive. Thus, science began within the cultural framework of a Christian worldview and its assumptions about the nature and meaning of life.

FUNDAMENTAL ASSUMPTIONS

Biblical religion and Western culture make certain fundamental assumptions about the material world.[12] First of all, the Bible teaches that nature is real. Hinduism teaches that the world of everyday material objects is illusion, merely "appearances" of the One, the Absolute, the Infinite. What would motivate one to study nature that is only an illusion?

Secondly, the Bible teaches that nature is of great value. The famous refrain, "And God saw that it was good," is repeated six times in the first chapter of Genesis. The philosophy of Plato and Aristotle lacked this basic understanding. Rather, Greek philosophy had a dualistic view of reality, which saw the realm of the spirit as far more important than the realm of the earthly, the realm of evil and disorder. Slaves did the manual labor; philosophers had more important matters to think about. How in the world could empirical science, with its focus on the creation and hands-on experimentation and observation, develop if matter was beneath the concern of the brightest and most learned Greeks?

The first scientists saw things quite differently. Nature was "godly." In one of his notebooks, the early astronomer, Johannes Kepler, prayed,

> I give you thanks, Creator and God, that you have given me this joy in thy creation, and I rejoice in the work of your hands. See, I have now completed the work to which I was called. In it I have used the talents you have lent to my spirit.[13]

Thirdly, the Bible teaches that nature, though it is good, is not god. Animism, the most common primitive religion, holds that spirits or gods reside in nature. The pagan man, in the words of Harvey Cox, "lives in an enchanted forest."[14] Nature is full of sun gods, river gods, star gods, mountain gods and wind gods. Ravines, streams, rocks and woods are filled with spirits, sprites, trolls, demons, dryads.

Conversely, Biblical religion constantly speaks against the idolatry and sacred groves of pagan worship. This desacralization of nature was crucial to the rise of science. How can you cut down a tree that may be inhabited by a spirit who will take revenge? How can you examine a rock whose spirit dislikes such an unwelcome invasion of its privacy? Nancy Pearcey and Charles Thaxton, in their great book, *The Soul of Science*, put it like this,

> The monotheism of the Bible exorcised the gods of nature, freeing humanity to enjoy and investigate without fear. When the world was no longer an object of worship, then – and only then – could it become an object of study.[15]

Fourth, the Bible teaches that the world is a place guided by intentional "laws." The first chapter of Genesis tells of a lawful creation in which everything has its assigned function (e.g., "Let there be lights ... and let them serve as signs to make seasons, and days, and years"), everything reproduces according to God's designated plan (e.g., "Let the waters teem with living creatures and let birds fly across the expanse of the sky. So God created the great creatures of the sea and every living and moving thing with which the waters teem, according to their kinds, and every winged creature according to its kind") and God's long-range plan is being fulfilled (e.g., "God blessed them and said, 'Be fruitful and increase in number and fill the water in the seas, and let the birds increase on the earth'"). Copernicus said he knew that the universe was "wrought for us by a supremely good and orderly creator."[16] The early scientists believed that order was a part of the character of God.

Melvin Calvin, a Nobel Prize-winning biochemist, says this:

> As I try to discern the origin of that conviction [that the universe is ordered], I sense to find it in the basic notion discovered 2,000 or 3,000 years ago ... by the ancient Hebrews: namely, that the universe is governed by a single God, and is not the product of the whims of many gods, each governing his own province according to his own laws. This monotheistic view seems to be the historical foundation for modern science.[17]

People in pagan cultures are unfamiliar with the idea that nature is governed by laws. Historian Carl Becker explains that, until the scientific revolution began, people did not generally see nature as lawful or rational but as mysterious and capricious. Christian teachers, however, said, "since God is goodness and reason, His creation must somehow be, even if not evidently so to finite minds, good and reasonable."[18] Thus, the laws of nature followed logically from the character of God.

Early scientists believed that the universe was an ordered creation that could be understood by rational minds. Science grew from the fertile ground of the Christian faith.

THE FAITH OF THE EARLY SCIENTISTS

As if it were not enough that the first science developed in a Christian culture, in *For the Glory of God* Rodney Stark includes a list of 52 scientists from nine European countries who were born approximately between 1500 and 1700. In selecting these scientists, he picked only those who made significant contributions. Copernicus is first on the list, historically. Most came from England, France, Italy and Germany. Half turned out to be Protestant, half Roman Catholic. Almost a third were clergymen.

After examining their writings, Stark classified 61.5 percent as devout Christians, 34.7 percent as "conventionally religious" and 3.8 percent as skeptics; that is, only two of these 52 scientists were not Christians. Stark's conclusion: "Were there any remaining doubt about it, these data make it entirely clear that religion played a substantial role in the rise of science."[19]

Isaac Newton is often credited with being the first true scientist. According to Newton, the physical world was explicable in terms of "insurmountable and uniform natural laws" that could be discovered by observation and formulated mathematically. The beauty and variety of the system, Newton believed, was irrefutable evidence that it had been designed by an intelligent and powerful Creator.[20]

COPERNICUS AND GALILEO

But what about Copernicus and Galileo? Both experienced the disapproval of the Church in their scientific pursuits. Didn't their experiences with church leaders prove the implacable hostility of Christianity toward science? No.

In the case of Copernicus, his training at the Catholic universities of his day (Krakow, Bologna, Padua and Ferrara) was without parallel. Moreover, the notion that the earth circles the sun did not come to him out of the blue; rather, "Copernicus was taught the essential fundamentals leading to the heliocentric model by his scholastic professors."[21]

The heliocentric model of the solar system rejected the notion that the earth was the center of the universe and, instead, postulated that the planets revolved around the sun. For 200 years, various scholastic teachers had progressed toward this understanding. It was primarily objected to, not by the use of Biblical references, but by quotations from Aristotle.

Expressing this fact in mathematics, which was to become the native tongue of science, was Copernicus' chief contribution. He was simply involved in the advance of knowledge in his day. Nothing in the Bible spoke against his theory that the earth went around the sun, and many contemporary scholastics at Catholic universities had already reached the same conclusion.

The story of Galileo is more of a textbook case of religious persecution. Still, there was more involved in Galileo's case than a simple conflict between science and religion. The fact is, most Church intellectuals were on Galileo's side, while his opposition came mainly from those who held secular, Aristotelian ideas. Even the pope had once been one of Galileo's followers. Galileo's problems with the Church had more to do with internal politics than with the Bible. Above all, they had to do with Galileo's decision to publish his works in the vernacular language rather than Latin, which the Church took to be a deliberate affront by its appeal to a wider reading public.

In spite of the conflict, Galileo never repudiated his faith.[22] Pearcey and Thaxton conclude Galileo's story with these words,

> To be true to history, we must take seriously Galileo's own protestations that he was a genuine Christian believer who had no intention of questioning religious doctrine *per se*, but only the scientific framework inherited from Aristotelian philosophy.[23]

Until recent years, Galileo's conflict with the Catholic Church has been largely mischaracterized by historians.

EVOLUTION

Even though the great ideas of the Christian faith gave birth to science, many in the late 19th and 20th centuries argued that the Christian faith was the enemy of science. Specifically, they argued that this was true in the case of the most dominant scientific theory of modern times – the theory of evolution.

Charles Darwin's *The Origin of Species* was published in 1859. Over the next 50 years, there was very little objection to Darwin's theories from Christian circles. The Biblical account makes it clear that creation, as the Bible calls it, was gradual. For years, theologians had not felt bound to believe that the six days of creation were 24-hour days. Even the most inexperienced reader of Genesis 1 can see that the word "day" in Genesis 2:4 ("In the day that the Lord God made the heavens and the earth ...") does not mean a single 24-hour day but a general period of time. Why, then, should we be obliged to believe that the word "day" in the previous verse means anything different?

John Calvin, the founding theologian of the Presbyterian Church, who lived at the time of the Protestant Reformation in the 1500s, certainly did not believe that the six days of creation were six literal days.[24]

It was, in fact, the so-called fundamentalist-modernist movement of the early 20th century that first made an issue of the matter, defining the six days of creation as six, 24-hour days. Prior to that, the length of time in view in Genesis 1 was never a "hot" theological issue. Many Christians, of course, believed that creation took place in six literal days, but many conservative theologians had taken the longer view. As late as the end of the 19th century, James McCosh, president of Princeton University and a devout Christian, embraced the view that evolution was simply the means by which God created all that is living on earth.[25]

If the word "day" used in Genesis 1-2 is non-specific, there is no impediment to the scientific understanding that the world is five billion years old, nor that the universe as a whole is 15 billion years old. In fact, however, those time periods are of rather recent scientific origin and certainly were not anything that Darwin had in view. As recently as the mid-20th century, there were still scientists who believed that the universe had been around forever, that matter was eternal. They held a view of the universe called the "Steady State" theory. It was only in the 1950s and 1960s that most scientists came to believe in the "Big Bang" theory. That theory says that matter is not eternal; rather, the universe began at a particular point in time about 15 billion years ago. At that time, a "singularity" – a tiny, incredibly dense piece of matter the size of the head of a pin – exploded to form the whole universe as we now know it. The theory says that we are living in a universe of several hundred billion galaxies, which is still expanding.

The conflict between evolution and the Christian faith began when devotees of evolution, such as Thomas Huxley (1825-1895), set evolution forth as an alternative to the Christian faith. Although refutation of the Christian faith is not a necessary result of Darwin's theory of evolution by natural selection, Huxley and others used Darwinism to propound "scientific atheism."[26] In the boast of Richard Dawkins, "Darwin made it possible to be an intellectually fulfilled atheist."[27]

Thus, it is very important to make a clear distinction between "Evolution" with a capital "E" – the idea that there is no God and natural evolution is the whole explanation of origins – and "evolution" with a small "e" – the idea that the world as we know it came to be through a long process of development over a period of time. The latter definition leaves open the role of God in that process and makes no implied faith statement that God was not involved.

But back to Darwin: The problem with *The Origin of Species* is that it never solved the problem of how species originate. In spite of the early openness of Christian theologians to the possibility that evolution might, if substantiated, be a description of how God created the world, some scientists have become, if anything, less convinced that Darwin's theory of natural selection has sufficient scientific basis. The problems with the theory have been growing over the years and include:

1. The absence of any scientific consensus on how life began in the first place.

2. The absence of many transitional forms (between species) in the fossil record.

3. The continued inability of scientists to cross species "barriers" in scientific experimentation.

4. The absence of an adequate explanation for the apparent beauty and design of nature.

5. The incredible odds against life arising and developing by chance (natural selection) over a very limited span of time.

6. The difficulty of explaining the riddle of how human consciousness could arise from an unconscious universe.

7. The lack of explanation for how species could arise all at once, which is what the fossil record shows. In fact, in the Cambrian period, all of the families (*phyla*) of species in the animal kingdom appear all at once over a very brief evolutionary period.

Unfortunately, most contemporary public discussions of this topic are freighted with a lot of emotion, in part due to mass confusion over Evolution and evolution. As a result, an either/or mentality has hardened within opposing camps, impeding a more thoughtful consensus from developing. Part of the problem is that Evolution is the "only game in town" when it comes to a scientific explanation for how life developed on earth. Another is that science, by nature, must look for naturalistic explanations, thus making a tacit assumption that naturalistic explanations are the whole story.

The brave face sometimes exhibited by scientists to the public on the subject of Evolution, however, does not necessarily represent their conversations with each other.

The ironic situation seems to be that while many conservative theologians seem willing to accept some kind of theory of the gradual emergence of life over billions of years, some scientists seem less sure than ever before that Evolution, unguided by God, is the whole story.[28]

In fact, it could be argued that every scientist believes in miracles. There used to be two alternative answers to the question, "What is it that has existed forever?" One was the Christian answer, "God." The other was the atheistic answer, "Matter" (because of the "Steady State" theory). Now, since the general acceptance of the "Big Bang" theory, "Matter" has been virtually eliminated as a valid response, and one is left staring at the question, "Who lit the fuse of that spectacular initial explosion?" If you believe in the "Big Bang," you believe in miracles. If you believe in miracles, you believe in some kind of God.

In his engaging book, *A Short History of Nearly Everything*, secular author Bill Bryson has written a masterpiece on the question of how we all got here. *The New York Times Book Review* on the book's front jacket is quoted saying that the book is "destined to become a modern classic of science writing." And it has. Bryson's introduction begins,

> Welcome. And congratulations. I am delighted you could make it. Getting here wasn't easy, I know. In fact, I suspect it was a little tougher than you realize. ... To begin with, for you to be here now trillions of drifting atoms had somehow to assemble in an intricate and intriguingly obliging manner to create you. ... Why atoms take this trouble is a bit of a puzzle. ... For all their devoted attention, your atoms don't actually care about you – indeed, they don't even know that you are there. They don't even know that they are there. They are mindless particles after all, and not even themselves alive. (It is a slightly arresting notion that if you were to pick yourself apart with tweezers, one atom at a time,

you would produce a mound of fine atomic dust, none of which had ever been alive but all of which had once been you. ...) The only thing special about the atoms that make you is that they make you. That, of course, is the miracle of life."[29]

The miracle of life! Bryson goes on using miraculous words, words implying that life, indeed, is a miracle. "To be here now," he says, "alive in the twenty-first century and smart enough to know it, you also had to be the beneficiary of an extraordinary string of good fortune."[30] Good fortune! Miraculous words pepper his sentences: "lucky," "miraculous," "fortunate," "astoundingly."

Scientists have no answer to the question of how life began. It is a miracle! They have not replicated it in the laboratory. Life began within an extraordinarily brief period of time in cosmic history. It didn't have forever, as we have so often been told. So large is this problem that some scientists have speculated that this earth was "seeded" with life from another planet elsewhere in the universe! However wild that speculation may be, it begs the question, "How did life begin on *that* planet?"

There are miracles everywhere. What about the Cambrian explosion – the sudden, concurrent appearance of all of the *phyla* (families) of the animal kingdom? What about the new evidence of probability theory, which says that to claim that the existence of life on earth is by chance is like saying that a tornado in a junkyard assembled itself into a giant 747 jet plane by chance. Or it is like claiming that a monkey sitting down at a typewriter, given enough time, could write the plays of Shakespeare by chance. The response used to be that, given enough time, it *could happen*, but now, probability theory says it couldn't. One commentator has explained it like this:

> Even if one makes the wild assumption that life came here from a much older faraway planet, the progression from simple to complex life-forms on Earth took place within a quite limited time. Even more telling is the fact that when competent mathematicians considered the matter, they quickly calculated that even if the monkey's task were reduced to coming up with only a few lines of *Macbeth*, let alone Shakespeare's entire play, the probability is far, far beyond any possibility. The odds of creating even the simplest organism at random are even more remote – Fred Hoyle and Chandra Wickramasinghe calculated the odds as 1 in $10^{40,000}$ (consider that all of the atoms in the

known universe are estimated to number no more than 10^{80}). In this sense, then, Darwinian theory does rest on truly miraculous assumptions.[31]

In this subject, there simply are "miracles" everywhere. And to believe in miracles is to believe in God. The Apostle Paul says in Romans 1, speaking of mankind in general:

> For what can be known about God is plain to them because God has shown it to them. Ever since the creation of the world His invisible nature, namely, His eternal power and deity, has been clearly perceived in the things that have been made. So they are without excuse; for although they knew God, they did not honor Him as God or give thanks to Him, but became futile in their thinking and their senseless minds were darkened.[32]

Could it be that the real issue behind a theory of evolution that leads to atheism (Evolution with a capital "E") is not the evidence of evolution but an unwillingness to acknowledge God and bow down in worship before Him?

WHY SCIENCE DID NOT ARISE IN OTHER CULTURES

In concluding this chapter, it is important to summarize briefly the fact that science arose only in the Judeo-Christian[33] culture of Western Europe and not in other cultures of the world. Why is it that science – with its method of theory, observation/ experimentation, revised theory – did not occur in other cultures as a method for understanding the natural world and how it operates? We have already considered why it arose in a culture with a Christian perspective, but why did it not occur in cultures with other perspectives?

Many religions and philosophies of the world simply had no interest in understanding the physical world and how it operates. Greek dualism saw the physical world as unworthy of the attention of philosophers. Hinduism and Buddhism sought to escape the physical world and its sufferings, not study it.

Other religions, like Confucianism and Taoism, were essentially moral codes that did not attempt to explain the origins or nature of this world. Religions involving animism, polytheism, the deification of matter or reincarnation saw nature as inhabited by spirits who were to be placated, rather than dissected. If the sacred cows of Hinduism could not be slaughtered for food, they certainly could not be dissected for science.

Finally, religions such as Islam had no creation story and, therefore, no beginning framework for the study of matter and nature. The Muslim problem has been put this way:

> It would seem that Islam has the appropriate God to underwrite the rise of science. But that's not so. Allah is not presented as a lawful creator but has been conceived of as an extremely active God who intrudes on the world as he deems it appropriate. Consequently, there soon arose a major theological bloc within Islam that condemned all efforts to formulate natural laws as blasphemy insofar as they denied Allah's freedom to act. That is, Islam did not fully embrace the notion that the universe ran along on fundamental principles laid down by God at the Creation, but assumed that the world was sustained by his will on a continuing basis. This was justified by a statement in the Qur'an: "Verily, God will cause to err whom he pleaseth, and will direct whom he pleaseth." Although the line refers to God's determination of the fate of individuals, it has been interpreted broadly to apply to all things. If God does as he pleases, and what he pleases is variable, the universe may not be lawful.[34]

CONCLUSION

It is the Christian faith, and the Christian faith alone, that provided the philosophical basis out of which science grew. That philosophical basis, or "great idea," is that God created the world; that the world existed first in the mind and plan of God, running according to rules that are discoverable; that the world, therefore, is other than Himself; that He created it good; that He gave man dominion over it and the power to "name" its creatures. He gave us two books in which to see His glory – the Bible and creation. Christians believed that they were following in His footsteps and getting to know Him better by committing themselves to the study of either. Thus, science began.

CHAPTER THREE

CHRISTIANITY AND THE IDEA OF THE UNIVERSITY

Tom Wolfe's novel, *I Am Charlotte Simmons*,[1] opens with a statement about the work of Victor Ransome Starling, a fictitious assistant professor of psychology at fictitious Dupont University. Starling received the Nobel Prize in biological sciences in 1997 for an experiment in which brain surgery was performed on 30 cats.

The surgery resulted in such oversexualization that the cats would form "daisy chains" of copulation "as long as ten feet." An additional control group of 30 cats watched all these goings-on and, when released from their cages, they proceeded to act in exactly the same way. Wolfe concludes that "Starling had discovered that a strong social order or 'cultural atmosphere,' even as abnormal as this one, could in time overwhelm the genetically determined responses of perfectly normal, healthy animals."

Enter Charlotte Simmons, a healthy, perfectly normal – albeit brilliant – girl from the hills of western North Carolina, who goes off to Dupont University on a Presidential Scholarship and gets swallowed up in an alcoholic, highly sexualized and politicized university culture. With a perfect 1600 on the SAT and a high score of "5" on four different Advanced Placement exams, Charlotte has been looking forward to experiencing "the life of the mind"[2] at Dupont.

Early in the book, however, she comes to understand that "the life of the mind" at a university today is more rare than she could possibly have imagined. Gradually, she comes to see students around her as "merely conscious little rocks,"[3] swept along by the decidedly non-mental preoccupations, immaturities and addictions of university life. In contrast, she sees herself as different and self-determined, a participant in the "life of the mind" with solid moral values to support it. "I am Charlotte Simmons" is the refrain that expresses that staunch individuality again and again in her thoughts throughout the better part of the book. In the end, however, she discovers that even she is not strong enough to resist the corruption of university life – and, ultimately, of the university itself.

Universities, though, were not always like this.

THE MEANING OF 'UNIVERSITY'

"University" comes from the Latin "*universus*," meaning "all together."[4] The word originally celebrated the fact that truth in its many aspects is ultimately one (thus, the prefix "*uni*" from the Latin "*unus*," meaning "one").

The great idea upon which universities were originally built is a Western, Christian idea. It is the understanding that *truth is one because all truth is God's truth* and, therefore, no area of knowledge is to be shunned or feared. All truths are related in a coherent whole in the mind of God the Creator. As science drew its origin from the Christian conviction that the world was created by God and, therefore, made sense, so the university found its origin in the conviction that all knowledge in God's universe is related and, therefore, to be welcomed.

The statement in Scripture that undergirds this perspective more than any other is Jesus' word to the Jews in the Gospel of John:

> If you continue in my Word, you are truly my disciples, and you will know the truth and the truth will make you free.[5]

On old college buildings, the second half of that statement is often carved in stone, but the first half is omitted. That omission is called "quoting out of context." It is unethical to proudly emblazon, "You will know the truth and the truth will make you free," on a seal or building while ignoring the clause on which it is conditioned: "If you continue in my Word, you are truly my disciples ..." The point, of course, is that it is the Word of Jesus Christ, and the consequent way of discipleship outlined in His teaching, that leads to truth and to freedom.

The earliest university professors of the Middle Ages believed this. The idea of the university made sense as a celebration of the oneness of truth in the midst of its many subjects. As one commentator states:

> Christianity depicted God as a rational, responsive, dependable and omnipotent being, and the universe as His personal creation, thus having a rational, lawful, stable structure awaiting human comprehension.[6]

Speaking of the early New England universities founded in the 1600s and 1700s, George Marsden, a professor of history at Notre Dame University, has made the same point in these words:

> The truths learned from Scripture and those learned from nature were assumed to be complementary. Christians who had long learned from the pagans could learn even more from their own natural philosophers. And since the creator of heaven and earth was also the author of Scripture, truths learned through the methods of philosophy and those learned from Biblical authority would supplement each other and harmonize in one curriculum.[7]

The late Richard John Neuhaus, former editor of *First Things,* criticizes the Smithsonian's National Museum of the American Indian because the general public is permitted to view only some of the collection, while the rest may only be seen by members of a specific tribe. Neuhaus quotes the museum director's explanation: the tribes know their culture, the artifacts are theirs and we must respect their concerns. But Neuhaus disagrees:

> The more important point is that the very idea of the modern museum is founded on a distinctly Western belief that knowledge is universal and a distinctly Western eagerness to learn from other cultures.[8]

That Western perspective came from the Christian faith. In many religions, the assertions and perspectives of other religions are to be feared and, therefore, are taboo. Anything that disagrees is "new" and "strange" and cannot be learned or weighed or considered because it is "foreign." Not so the Christian faith.

In our own time, scientists have sought to discover the unified field theory – or "theory of everything" – that unites the four forces of nature:

electro-magnetism, gravity, the strong nuclear force and the weak nuclear force. In fact, the great English physicist Stephen Hawking has gone so far as to say that finding this Holy Grail of science would mean the ability to predict all events in the universe.[9] The early universities, both in Europe and America, had a different but similar grand thought – the integration of all truth.

This unified vision of truth implies a "liberal" vision in the old sense of that word, where every idea may be expressed, every discovery shared and every theory run the gauntlet of falsification or confirmation. It is a vision of truth as objective and non-contradictory, not as a subjective understanding of different, mutually exclusive perspectives ("That's not the way I see it") or therapeutic uses ("If it helps, it's true for me"). It is a vision that understands that the heart of truth, the theory of everything in different garb, has already been revealed by God in Scripture. There is, therefore, no fear in the pursuit of truth. All paths and all subjects are open; freedom of inquiry prevails. Vigorous discussion in the marketplace of ideas is made possible by Christian foundations. All truth is God's truth.

MEDIEVAL UNIVERSITIES

In much the same way that the early scientists believed in God's two books – the book of His Word (the Bible) and the book of His works (Creation), both of which were fit objects of study to His glory – so the early university professors believed that ancient classical learning contained truth. It was included under a concept called "natural theology" (the provision of glimpses of God's truth in nature)[10] and "common grace" (understandings of God given graciously to all).[11]

At the end of the first millennium, early universities were called "scholastic" universities because of their devotion to classical Greek learning, as well as to the Bible and Christian tradition. Any rediscovery of classical knowledge that took place in the Middle Ages took place through Christian influence.

They followed in the tradition of the Irish monks who fanned out across Europe in the 600s and 700s, bringing with them not only Scripture, but also classical Greek and Roman texts.[12] The monasteries they established became part of an early system that would become the scholastic universities of Europe in the late Middle Ages.[13]

All instruction was in Latin, and degrees were mutually recognized, so movement and cross-fertilization from one university to another took place within a structure of very few barriers. All scholars enjoyed the extra privileges of clerics. Cities and villages vied for the privilege of hosting a university and often paid the salaries of the professors.

Scholars gained prestige and promotion, not by simply retracing old territory, but by innovation – the same standard for doctoral work today. All of the Protestant Reformers, from Wycliffe and Hus to Calvin and Luther, were university scholars.

Since Greek, not Latin, was the language of classical times, many scholars knew Greek as well as Latin and, by the end of the 1100s, many Greek manuscripts had been translated into Latin. Rodney Stark comments,

> Notice that these translations of classical scholarship were not the work of Humanists rebelling against the "long night" of Christian ignorance. The rediscovery [of the Greek classics] was accomplished by exceedingly pious Christian scholars in their newly created universities.[14]

Scholars such as Albertus Magnus (1205-1280) studied not only the Aristotelian tradition of the operation of the universe – but also attempted to subject Aristotle's claims to observational testing.[15]

Furthermore, it was not the Greeks, the Romans, the Muslims or the Chinese who first dissected the human body for the purpose of medical knowledge. Scholastics at early Christian universities initiated this pursuit. As early as the 1200s, such procedures had become common.[16]

From the beginning, scholars at the universities of medieval Europe believed that all truth was God's truth and therefore, that truth when integrated, was non-contradictory. Various parts were assumed to relate to other parts and to the whole. The relation of reason to faith, the relation of science to theology, the relation of the Greek classics to the Bible and the church fathers – all were a part of a unified vision of truth from which no area of knowledge was excluded.

This openness meant that the universities of medieval times were largely open and free. Of course, they ultimately had to operate within the boundaries of the Church, but those boundaries – by any standard – were very broad. Freedom of inquiry was not feared. Instead, these universities were liberal (i.e., free) in a way that is not true of many modern secular universities which, nevertheless, proudly – but falsely – claim the mantle of "liberal education." Every subject was a fit object of inquiry and no subject was dangerous or beneath the dignity of scholars.

EARLY AMERICAN UNIVERSITIES

In 1636, just a few brief years after the Pilgrims landed in Massachusetts, Harvard University was founded. The earliest design for the Harvard seal, proposed in 1643, simply featured one word, "*veritas*" – "truth." The motto of the seal of the 1650 Harvard charter was "*In Christi gloriam*" – "in Christ's glory." The seal of the 1692 charter had the words "*Christo et ecclesiae*" – "for Christ and the church."[17]

One of Harvard's early presidents, Increase Mather, said in a commencement address at the end of the 1600s: "Find a friend in Plato, a friend in Socrates, but above all find a friend in truth."[18] In other words, narrowness was discouraged and breadth encouraged. The theological tradition of the Puritans embodied a concept familiar to the medieval scholastics, a concept of universal truth in which God, the Creator, was at the center and all pursuits of truth were open for exploration.

According to George Marsden in his book, *The Soul of the American University: From Protestant Establishment to Established Nonbelief*, the Puritan devotion to higher education "was for them a high priority in civilization building."[19] As a result, Marsden says:

> By establishing a college so early (in the southern colonies, it
> took a century to do the same), the Puritans laid the foundation
> for New England's dominance in American higher education
> for the next three centuries. As late as the era when Americans
> founded modern universities, or transformed their colleges
> into universities, few of the key leaders lacked New England
> connections. [20]

Eighty-four years after the founding of Harvard, Yale College was founded in 1720 in New Haven, Connecticut as a Puritan, Protestant institution. By this time, theological orthodoxy at Harvard was considered to be in decline. To ensure orthodoxy, Yale required all officers of the college to subscribe to the Westminster Confession of Faith. [21] The motto adopted by Yale was "*veritas et lux*" – "truth *and* light" – a not-so-subtle dig at Harvard's original motto, "*veritas*." Jonathan Edwards, perhaps the greatest of early American theologians, was a Yale student.

Yale's evangelical perspective continued for 200 years. Dwight L.

Moody, one of the great American evangelists of the 19th century, was elected to the Yale board of trustees in 1878. At that time, the trustees were still mostly clergy and, like the faculty, were required to be members of an evangelical church.[22]

In 1746 the College of New Jersey, later Princeton University, was founded. Originally, a majority of Princeton's trustees were Presbyterian clergy of an evangelical persuasion.[23] Its presidents continued to be Presbyterians and orthodox Christians through the tenures of James McCosh and Francis Patton. Patton, a Presbyterian minister, taught at Princeton Seminary before becoming president in 1888, following McCosh. He served until 1902.[24]

After Princeton, a succession of new clergy-founded colleges followed in quick succession: Columbia in 1754, Pennsylvania in 1755, Brown in 1764, Rutgers in 1766 and Dartmouth in 1769. All remained Christian colleges until the turn of the 20th century.

The point of this history is not to suggest that all contemporary colleges and universities should require their faculty to subscribe to a doctrinal statement or enforce a litmus test of Christian belief. It is to suggest that, to the degree the modern university eschews the Christian faith, it has strayed from the philosophical underpinnings that gave rise to, and ultimately still support, full and free academic inquiry.

AMERICAN UNIVERSITIES IN THE 20TH CENTURY

Around 1900, a change began to take place in American universities. By the end of the century, almost without exception, all had been dramatically altered. What had once been an educational system that cherished its Christian history had become a system which, if anything, had an animus against Christianity. Gone were the openness and freedom of truly liberal education. Many opinions had become unacceptable; the great books of Western civilization had been re-envisioned as the biased and self-serving works of "dead white males" and many subjects became dominated by the need to come up with the "right" answers, rather than openness to research.

In January, 2005 Harvard President Larry Summers made a speech at a "Diversifying the Science and Engineering Workforce" conference, in which he said that the lack of women in science in American universities should be researched, including research into possible scientific aptitude disparities between men and women.

There was nothing strange about this suggestion. A significant amount of current research exists on natural differences between men and women, the differences in the way their minds develop, and the existence of genetic differences in mental approach and capacity in general.[25] Nevertheless, a firestorm of protest erupted that forced Summers to apologize repeatedly, though there was really nothing for which to apologize. He was accused of "sexism," an unpardonable sin. Summers resigned just one year later, stating he had lost the confidence of the faculty.

In March, 2005 Jada Pinkett Smith, wife of actor Will Smith, received the "Artist of the Year Award" from the Harvard Foundation. In her acceptance speech, she spoke about overcoming the significant disadvantage of being the child of heroin addicts. In speaking of her present happiness, she said:

> Women, you can have it all – a loving man, a devoted husband, loving children, a fabulous career. ... To my men, open your mind, open your eyes to new ideas, be open.[26]

Not bad advice for students at a liberal university: Be open to the pursuit of truth at any cost. Well, not any cost. One of the campus groups affiliated with the Foundation, the Bisexual, Gay, Lesbian, Transgender and Supporters Alliance (BGLTSA), found her words "extremely heteronormative" and, moreover, said she "made BGLTSA members feel uncomfortable." The BGLTSA, according to an editorial in the *Wall Street Journal*, had earlier brought it to the university's attention "that bathrooms labeled 'men' and 'women' can create an atmosphere of hostility and fear for some people."

The Harvard Foundation dutifully apologized for Ms. Smith's remarks and promised to make sure it wouldn't happen again. Implying what? Censorship of acceptance speeches? So much for the open pursuit of truth at Harvard – an apparently illiberal, un-open, un-free academic institution at the pinnacle of American culture.

RELATIVISM AND THE PURSUIT OF TRUTH

In his well-known book, *The Closing of the American Mind: How Higher Education Has Failed Democracy and Impoverished the Souls of Today's Students*, Allan Bloom, a professor of social thought at the University of Chicago, begins with these words:

> There is one thing a professor can be absolutely certain of:
> almost every student entering the university believes, or says
> he believes, that truth is relative. If this belief is put to the
> test, one can count on the student's reaction: they will be
> uncomprehending. That anyone should regard the proposition
> as not self-evident astonishes them, as though he were calling
> into question $2 + 2 = 4$.[27]

The old saying on college campuses today is that there are no absolutes, except for one: "There are no absolutes." So much for the pursuit of truth, which, after all, is what a liberal education is supposed to be all about. And we're talking here about anecdotal reports from Harvard University and the University of Chicago, two of the most prestigious institutions in the country.

There can be no genuine pursuit of truth when relativism prevails. If everything is relative, then there is no truth to pursue. And there can be no genuine pursuit of truth where research suggestions are rejected out of hand because they might offend somebody, as was the case with Larry Summers' suggestion.

The fact is, the pursuit of truth in whole fields of university-level study has been warped by political bias. Let me give two brief examples.

The study of homosexuality has been derailed by the prevalence of five political myths:

1. **Homosexuals comprise 10 percent of the population.** An erroneous figure from Alfred Kinsey, one of the first academics to research sexual behavior, current statistics indicate that self-identified male homosexuals comprise only 2-3 percent of the male population – and the percentage of lesbians is even smaller.[28]

2. **Homosexuality is genetically determined.** It is not, though it may be influenced by genetic factors, as alcoholism is.

3. **Homosexuality is an either/or proposition – either one "really" is a homosexual or one is not.** Anyone who has had a single homosexual thought is often defined as "really" a homosexual. In fact, there is a broad spectrum between exclusive homosexuality and exclusive heterosexuality. Most "homosexuals" and "lesbians" are actually bisexual to some degree and often have experienced heterosexual arousal and intercourse.

4. **There is no movement on the orientation spectrum, and therefore, therapy cannot alter orientation.** Dr. Robert Spitzer, a psychiatrist who led the movement to remove homosexuality from the *Diagnostic and Statistical Manual of Mental Disorders*, recently completed a study of 227 former homosexuals who responded successfully to reorientation therapy. Through that study, Spitzer became convinced that reorientation to heterosexuality is possible.[29] Though many people, for philosophical or political reasons, object to attempts at reorientation such bias should not obscure the truth that reorientation can occur.

5. **Homosexuals are "gay."** In fact, many are sad. Homosexuals have suicide rates, disease rates, alcoholism rates, drug addiction rates and incidence of mental-health problems that are much higher than in the population at large. So serious are these problems cumulatively that the life expectancy of active male homosexuals is significantly less than that of the population as a whole.[30]

These five myths fly in the face of the best science on the subject of homosexuality. Yet where in university life today can one find any serious debate on the issue? Political considerations have trumped the best science, and the basic truths about homosexuality remain largely unknown.

As a second example, the study of Western civilization at Yale experienced a serious setback when two graduates, Lee and Perry Bass, offered to give $20 million to the university to endow a program on Western civilization. The faculty wouldn't consider it and, after years of wrangling, the money was ultimately withdrawn. The problem? Yale's faculty saw the gift as an invasion of their turf. They had no interest, moreover, in supporting a program on the history of Western civilization.[31]

The "truth problem" in university life today was described by recent Yale president Benno Schmidt:

> The most serious problems of freedom of expression in our society today exist on our campuses. ... The assumption seems to be that the purpose of education is to induce correct opinion rather than to search for wisdom and liberate the mind.[32]

FREE SPEECH

A recent book by Mike S. Adams, *Welcome to the Ivory Tower of Babel: Confessions of a Conservative College Professor*, describes his first-hand account of a clash with the "thought police" of the diversity movement at the University of North Carolina-Wilmington:

> Some call this the multi-cultural era on our nation's campuses.
> Others call it the post-modern era. I call it chaos because
> everyone seems to be speaking a different language. And, sadly,
> there is little interest in universal truths or principles in academia
> today.[33]

One week after the September 11th terrorist attacks, Adams received an e-mailed statement from a former student entitled, "In Dedication to an Undivided Humanity." In this piece, blame for the attack was not assigned to the hijackers or to Osama Bin Laden – but to the government of the United States. The statement claimed that "the U.S. is seen by tens of millions [across the world] as the main enemy of their human and democratic rights and the main source of their oppression," and further claimed that "the American ruling elite, in its insolence and cynicism, acts as if it can carry out its violent enterprises around the world without creating the conditions for violent retribution."[34]

Adams replied that the lengthy statement was "undeserving of serious consideration." He called it "an intentionally divisive diatribe." Adams further advised that, though "the Constitution protects your speech just as it has protected bigoted, unintelligent and immature speech for many years," nevertheless the former student needed to know that when she exercised her free speech rights in this way she was opening herself up "to criticism that is protected by the same principle."[35]

Adams was only one of a list of people who had received the same e-mail. He was angry. Two of his friends in New York City were still missing in the aftermath of September 11. This was a heartfelt loss for him. His response was only one short paragraph.

Four days later, he received a phone call from the university provost telling him the student had filed an official complaint against him and was threatening to sue him for libel.[36] Further, the written complaint demanded that all e-mails sent by Adams on university computers be opened to inspection by her representatives.

The university handled the situation badly and did, in fact, inspect Adams' e-mail on the basis of this bizarre First Amendment complaint. In the end, Adams won complete vindication. This should not have been a First Amendment issue, but cases like this have the effect of intimidating honest and forthright speech. No one wants to be threatened with a court case.

DIVERSITY

Adams also discusses at length how the mantra of diversity has run amok at his university. While the university already had an Office of Campus Diversity with a director and a full-time staff, a diversity "task force" under the authority of the chancellor distributed a report recommending the creation of the position of "Associate Provost of Diversity." Diversity is a broad word for a focus on racial, sexual orientation, abortion and feminist issues. It does not refer to any genuine interest in diverse representation of opinion.

The university has an African-American Center, a Women's Center and a Gay and Lesbian Center. It also has separate black faculty meetings, separate women's faculty meetings and separate lunch meetings for black faculty and staff.

Very simply, the diversity movement divides the campus and provides a platform for the propagation of one sort of opinion on issues relating to race, sexual orientation, abortion and feminism. Adams quips: "Many, like myself, fear that their vision of progress will soon include separate water fountains."[37]

In contrast, the Christian faith not only welcomes others but welcomes an open discussion of truth with them. To the extent that the diversity movement encourages the separation of one class of people from others, it weakens the pursuit of truth. It injects fear, prejudice and distance into the academic community.

CHRISTIAN PERSECUTION

One of the most astonishing elements recounted by Adams is the amount of anti-Christian sentiment at the university. He says:

> Although I was a liberal and an atheist when I began teaching
> at UNC-Wilmington, I was taken aback by the prevalence of
> anti-Christian sentiment, as well as by the degree of comfort
> professors felt in expressing it both inside and outside the
> classroom.[38]

He recounts an incident in which a Christian student group at the University of North Carolina-Chapel Hill, InterVarsity Christian Fellowship, was threatened with loss of university recognition unless it allowed non-Christian students to serve as group officers. Loss of recognition by the University of North Carolina is no small matter. It denies the use of university facilities and access to university funding, effectively banning groups from campus.

In fact, the assistant director of Student Activities and Organizations had written similar letters to 17 groups, including Music Makers Christian Fellowship, Young Life, The Lutheran Campus Ministry and The Episcopal Campus Ministry. All of these groups had received the same ultimatum: You must include non-Christians; in fact, you must not use the word "Christian."[39]

InterVarsity Christian Fellowship joined with a well-funded outside Christian organization to fight its battle and, of course, won hands down. The threats were a clear violation of the First Amendment. It was a content-based restriction of speech and assembly aimed specifically at Christians, asking them to abandon their core religious beliefs and allow non-Christians to become leaders and members.

ATHEISM

Perhaps one of the most amazing things to take place on American university campuses between 1900 and 2000 is the transition from Christian conviction to atheism. At Princeton University, for example, the president in 1900 was a Christian and a clergyman. The current president (in the 21st century) is a self-described atheist.

There is a sense that atheism – or, at the very most, a private faith that can never be openly discussed – is now a requirement on many college campuses. The logic runs like this: If tolerance, diversity and relativism are the core values of university life, then one must take great pains to avoid religion, especially Christianity. One can never articulate an idea that might be considered "exclusivist" by somebody else. Dr. Jim Nelson Black, former executive director of the Wilberforce Forum and a senior policy analyst of Sentinel Research Associates in Washington, D.C., explains it like this:

> In other words, the liberal view insists that we have no grounds
> for determining what is true; therefore, any claim to truth must be
> discounted and disavowed. This means, of course, that religious
> beliefs which rely upon revelation and absolute standards of truth,
> have no place in the academy.[40]

As the title of an article in the *Harvard Political Review* puts it, "The most troubling bias among academics is not political but religious."[41]

Dr. Jim Nelson Black discusses one student who describes his college odyssey as that of an atheist who "was looking for a moral justification for life." In a high school AP class, his teacher described photosynthesis as a "symphony of work," a description the student thought magnificent. When he got to college, he sincerely believed everyone was going to be objective and not try to impose their worldview on the subject matter. No such luck!

Although neither conservative nor religious, he found himself defending basic common sense. The deck always seemed stacked. Only one side of an issue was usually presented, and the discussion always seemed to lead to the presenter's worldview. He realized that one political perspective controlled the meaning of diversity and racism – and the determination of right and wrong. In dorm discussions, students had to agree that homosexuality was okay but couldn't talk about anything religious, especially Christianity.

As he searched for meaning, he eventually concluded that there must be a God – nothing made sense without that. The absolute necessity of a belief in right and wrong finally tipped the balance. He said:

> I couldn't accept the fact that there was no right and wrong. And
> if there's right and wrong, then there has to be a creator who
> made it that way.[42]

But it was an uphill battle. One Zogby poll of college seniors found that 73 percent believe that "what is right and wrong depends on differences in individual values and cultural diversity."[43] This student understood that a relativistic framework – no divinely bestowed standards for human life – presupposes atheism.

As Dallas Willard, professor of philosophy at the University of Southern California describes, Nietzsche and his followers realized it wasn't enough to get rid of God: You have to get rid of truth, too. But if there is no truth, all reasoning becomes rationalization. Nietzsche, he says, is *the* great man on campus today:[44]

> The underlying premise of the modern academic enterprise is
> that something has been found out. Someone, somewhere has
> found out that there is no God, that the Bible is a made-up bunch
> of fiction, that no one really knows anything about truth, and this
> just infects the whole system. ... Nietzsche was right ... in saying

that this world cannot remain the same if you accept the idea that
God is dead.[45]

The atheism of many academics today inevitably influences the
academy in a specific and deleterious direction.

ALCOHOL AND SEX

According to the *Education Law Reporter*, 63 percent of college
students rank drinking as their favorite activity. The Center for Science
in the Public Interest says, "More of the nation's undergraduates will
ultimately die from alcohol-related causes than will go on to get master's
and doctoral degrees combined."[46] By all accounts, alcohol is one of the
great problems on college campuses today. But most universities, rejecting
the role of moral adviser, have done nothing significant to restrain drinking,
in general or binge drinking, in particular.

Perhaps more significant is the prominent role played by alcohol in
the sexual activity of college students. Seventy percent of sexually active
college students say that being under the influence of alcohol plays a
significant role in their behavior. A pamphlet from the national Centers for
Disease Control and Prevention (CDC) concludes that "STD heaven" is
the predictable result of mixing alcohol with young men and women away
from their parents for the first time.

Sexually transmitted diseases do flourish on university campuses. The
fastest growing population of people infected with HIV is teenagers and
young adults in college.[47] The list of STDs making the rounds includes at
least 25 separate diseases.

The CDC has called this crisis among high school and college students
a "multiple epidemic:" 20 percent have herpes; 33 percent of females have
the human papilloma virus, which causes 99.7 percent of cervical cancer
cases; and 10 percent have chlamydia. Half of all girls are likely to be
infected with an STD during their first sexual experience.[48]

The readily available alternative, of course, is premarital abstinence
and commitment to faithfulness in marriage.

CONCLUSION

Tom Wolfe had it right. Sex- and alcohol-related issues dominate
university life today. But, as important as they are, these two are only the
tip of the iceberg. Atheism prevails, and Christianity is shunned or feared

when it escapes from its private, personal, secret cage to become a part of open discussion. Too often, the search for truth is no longer open or actively pursued; instead, it is rejected as "exclusivist" and an inappropriate goal in a relativistic culture. Moral issues have been reduced to matters of political correctness.

The risk in a university that is truly liberal, truly open and truly welcoming of all knowledge is that it is vulnerable to the prejudices of those who don't know what the idea of the university is all about. Fledgling democracies are vulnerable to the pitfall of "one man, one vote, one time" – the idea that one's vote *can* be used to impose a dictatorship, obviate all future elections and put an end to democracy.

In the free flow of ideas that the true university allows exists the risk that some may want to use that openness to establish their own tyranny of ideas, excluding other ideas from discussion. Part of the reason Christianity disappeared from so many universities in the 20th century is simply that these universities lost the gamble of openness to those who did not understand or value a truly open education, wanting instead to use it for their own purposes, to advance their own ideas and, ultimately, to limit freedom of inquiry.

At many universities there is no longer an open forum for ideas. Demonstrations, not reason, have become a too frequent means of convincing others. Christianity is allowed but cannot be discussed. Faculty candidates who are "too religious" may be denied appointment without further discussion. Evolution (as the whole answer to the question of origins), homosexuality, relativism, androgyny and Christianity are all placed in a category labeled, "Not to be discussed." Quoting "there are no absolutes" elicits no smiles. It is no joking matter. It is the holy of holies.

The change in university life over the past 100 years is, in many ways, simply astonishing. The belief that new ideas are not to be feared because truth is one and all truth is God's truth has all but vanished. The result? Much worthwhile exploration and study of truth – what used to be called a "liberal" education – has disappeared from universities precisely because those who are truly open are not in leadership positions, nor are they welcomed there.

The irony is that many modern universities believe that Christians are closed to truth because they are bound by the "revelation" found in the Bible and, therefore, are prejudiced. What they fail to see is that the political correctness, and the devotion to trends within each discipline, found in many of their professors have made them far more closed to "new" truths than Christians. In my limited experience, it is Christian professors who read everything in their field and non-Christian professors whose reading is confined only to the *avant-garde* or those who are likeminded. In the academy, breadth of research should "win," but the prejudice of those afraid to be open to positions other than their own is strong.

Nevertheless, the beacon of the original concept of the university still shines across the years in the history and meaning of the term "university," encouraging professors to be open to truth and not to fear it. This is God's universe. The great idea of the Christian faith that gave rise to the university is that "truth is one, because all truth is God's truth." Every field of study became legitimate. The concept of a liberal education was born. And "the life of the mind" remains a noble and joyous pursuit.

CHAPTER FOUR

CHRISTIANITY AND THE ABOLITION OF SLAVERY

One of the most widely read early novels in America was *Uncle Tom's Cabin* by Harriet Beecher Stowe, published in 1852. When she paid a visit to the White House in the midst of the Civil War, President Lincoln remarked, "So you're the little woman who wrote the book that made this great war."[1] And there is no doubt that her book was not only widely read in the years running up to the Civil War, but it was also a significant factor in arousing public sentiment against slavery.

Stowe was the daughter and sister of two prominent 19th century clergymen, Lyman Beecher (1775-1863) and Henry Ward Beecher (1813-1887), both of whom played important roles in the abolitionist movement prior to the Civil War. In fact, abolitionist societies sprang up everywhere in the early 1800s, and clergymen played a prominent role in fueling their fires. Evangelist Charles Finney, probably the most famous of the era, founded Oberlin College in Ohio, and made it a key station in the "underground railroad" traveled by slaves escaping the South on a journey to freedom in Canada.[2]

Uncle Tom's Cabin is the story of a Christian slave named Uncle Tom who lives on a Kentucky plantation. Because of his great value, he is sold by his master in order to save the plantation from bankruptcy. At the same time, a little slave boy, between 4 and 5 years old, is also sold. As a result, the boy's mother, Eliza, runs away with the child before he can be delivered to his new owner. Unbeknownst to her, as she heads toward Canada that night, her husband, George, a slave on a neighboring plantation, precedes her by only a few days. Later, they are reunited.

The remainder of the book (fully 90 percent) follows these two sagas – Uncle Tom's journey from owner to owner, and Eliza and George's long journey to Canada with their little son, Harry.

The book highlights the breakup of families common in the American slave system, the Christian faith of many of the masters and slaves, the endearing relationships of some owner families with their slaves, the rank prejudice endemic to the system, the clergymen who preached for and against slavery, the slaves' deep longing for freedom and the terrible suffering of many slaves at the hands of cruel masters. In the end, Uncle Tom is beaten to death by his last and most infamous master, Simon Legree.

"Uncle Tom," by dictionary definition, has come to mean "a black whose behavior toward whites is regarded as fawning and servile."[3] This corruption of meaning is the result of popular confusion between being a servant and being servile. Stowe's Uncle Tom is anything but fawning and servile. In fact, he is beaten to death because he refuses to tell what he knows about the escape of two slaves. Rather, he represents a deeply devoted Christian slave, serving his masters according to the advice of the Apostle Paul in Ephesians:

> Slaves be obedient to your earthly masters, with fear and
> trembling, in singleness of heart, as to Christ; not in the way of
> eye-service, as men pleasers, but as servants of Christ, doing the
> will of God from the heart, rendering service with a good will as
> to the Lord and not to men, knowing that whatever good anyone
> does, he will receive the same again from the Lord, whether he is
> a slave or free.[4]

The phrase, "doing the will of God from the heart," means the service in view is within Christian moral bounds and does not call for betraying a fellow slave into capture and even death.

The book is a lengthy narrative of the Christian stance on slavery, pointing firmly toward abolition as the true Christian viewpoint.

At the book's end, the son of Uncle Tom's first master comes to Simon

Legree's plantation, intent on buying the old slave back and freeing him, only to find that Uncle Tom is at the point of death from his final beating. The son knocks out Simon Legree with his fist, takes Uncle Tom's body, buries it and, kneeling on the grave, prays to God saying, "Oh, witness that from this hour I will do what one man can do to drive out this curse of slavery from my land."[5]

ONLY IN CHRISTIANITY

Historically, sustained and transformative moral opposition to slavery came only from those of Christian conviction. There are, of course, references to Christian slave masters in the New Testament. Nevertheless, among the world's religions, only in Christianity did the idea emerge that slavery was against the will of God and must be abolished.[6]

How did this happen, and why is this so?

HISTORICAL CONTEXT

To facilitate an honest investigation of this subject, it seems necessary to establish a clear understanding of the facts. Let me begin by asking some questions that have unexpected answers.

Question: Is the phenomenon of slavery in America relatively rare in human history?

Answer: No, slavery has existed throughout the history of the world in virtually every culture that could afford it, until the modern anti-slavery movement.[7] Even the American Indians of the Northwest had slaves from conquered Indian tribes, who often made up as much as one-third of the population of some villages.[8]

Question: Were there slaves in Greece and Rome in classical times?

Answer: Yes, there were some periods in which slaves outnumbered the free populations of Greece and the Roman Empire.[9] Plato left five slaves in his will; Aristotle, 14.[10] Every household in Athens and Rome had slaves. Even low-ranking soldiers had a slave or two.[11]

Question: How did humanists in the age of the enlightenment treat the fact of widespread slavery in the times of these classical heroes?

Answer: Humanists were indifferent to the fact that these were slave societies. Many made excuses. Friedrich Engels, writing in 1878, said: "Without slavery, no Greek state, no Greek art and science." Most saw slavery as essential to the Greek devotion to spiritual considerations and the high culture of classical times. Their attitude was, "Slavery and its attendant loss of humanity were part of the sacrifice which had to be paid for this achievement."[12]

Question: It's well known that slavery among the Jews was severely restricted and among New Testament Christians was discouraged, but not disallowed. What about among Muslims?

Answer: Muslim slave trading began long before slaves came to the Americas and continues to this day in many places, such as Sudan. By 1600, it is estimated that more than seven million Africans had been taken into captivity by Muslims. The fundamental problem for Muslims on the subject of slave trading is that Muhammad, himself, bought, sold, captured and owned slaves.[13]

Question: Where did the word "slave" come from?

Answer: From the word "slav," referring to Slavic people, whom the Muslims enslaved in great numbers – probably totaling several million – from Eastern European countries in the latter half of the first millennium.[14]

Question: How many slaves were brought to the Americas?

Answer: From 1510 to 1868, about 10 million slaves were brought to the New World. Of the 10 million who reached the New World, probably 20 million started the journey, with about half dying on the way.[15]

Question: Did they all come to the United States?

Answer: Only about four percent (or 400,000) came to the United States. In contrast, about 750,000 were imported by Jamaica and 3.6 million by Brazil.[16]

Question: Did Americans start the African slave trade?

Answer: No. Long before the Americans arrived, slave trading was well established in Africa. The first African slaves were slaves of other Africans. American slave traders tapped into an already existing business.[17]

Question: When did the first slaves come to the United States?

Answer: The first black slaves arrived in New York City in 1626, brought in a Dutch ship to what was then New Amsterdam.[18]

Question: Were slaves confined to the southern states?

Answer: No. In 1790, due to their Puritan heritage, there were two states in which slavery was illegal: Massachusetts and Maine.[19] The Pilgrims who settled Massachusetts' Plymouth Colony in 1620 opposed slavery for Christian reasons from the beginning.

Question: Were there slaves, then, even in New York State?

Answer: Yes. In 1790, there were 21,193 slaves in New York State – 6.3 percent of the total population.[20]

Question: Were there many freed slaves before the Civil War?

Answer: Yes. In 1830, there were more than 28,000 freed slaves in New Orleans alone. Almost half the African Americans in New Orleans were free. Some owned plantations themselves, farmed by slaves. But that was a great exception.[21] Although every state had some freed slaves, they often made up only one or two percent of the African-American population.[22]

As early as the Middle Ages, there was virtually no slavery in Europe due to long-standing Christian influence. In fact, when the New World was first being populated, Pope Paul III decreed, "Indians and all other peoples … should not be deprived of their liberty or of their possessions … and are not to be reduced to slavery."[23]

The abolition of slavery did not come throughout the Western world until the 1800s:

> It was not philosophers or secular intellectuals who assembled the moral indictment of slavery, but the very people they held in such contempt: men and women having intense Christian faith, who opposed slavery because it was a sin.[24]

THE GREAT IDEA

So, in the 1800s, a great idea conquered the Western world and subsequently, by example, much of the rest of the world. The idea? That there is an inherent dignity in every human being because *all human beings are created in the image of God* or, put simply, "human beings have souls" because they were created by God for fellowship with Himself. He created them out of love to be His own beloved children. That is why the first and great commandment always has been:

> You shall love the Lord your God with all your heart, and with all your soul and with all your mind.[25]

And that is why the Old Testament speaks of the creation of man in these words:

> Then God said, "Let us make man in our image, after our likeness. … So God created man, in the image of God He created him, male and female He created them.[26]

In these two verses, the word "image" occurs three times and the word "likeness" once. The author could not have been more definite. Human beings are like God, given a dignity that, in the end, rules out slavery.

SLAVERY IN THE OLD TESTAMENT

It has sometimes been alleged by misguided religionists that the whole African race was condemned to slavery because of the so-called "sin of Canaan" when Ham, the son of Noah and the father of Canaan, looked upon the nakedness of his drunken father. When Noah awoke, he said, "Cursed be Canaan, a slave of slaves shall he be to his brothers."[27] Careful readers of this passage have rightly noted that there is no way to tell whether Canaan was specifically meant to stand for black people or for all of the generations of Canaan's descendants that followed him.

The Israelites were allowed to hold slaves,[28] but not from among their own people.[29] The fact that the Israelites were once slaves themselves was to moderate their attitude toward slaves. Regarding a slave, the Israelites were given this command, "You shall not rule over him with harshness, but shall fear your God."[30] Moreover, in the year of Jubilee (every 49 years) every slave or indentured servant was to be freed,[31] thereby curbing slavery.

SLAVERY IN THE NEW TESTAMENT

Some critics also suggest that the New Testament condones slavery. In fact, *Uncle Tom's Cabin* illustrates the fact that, prior to the Civil War, some Christian ministers preached against slavery and some for it. Slavery in the New Testament is not a simple issue.

It is true that the Apostle Paul encouraged slaves to obey their masters and serve them as if they were serving Christ, as noted previously. However, in that same passage and with equal force, Paul continues,

> Masters, do the same to them, and forbear threatening, knowing that He who is both their Master and yours is in heaven, and that there is no partiality with Him.[32]

In Colossians, Paul places masters in a role of servitude as fellow slaves of Christ:

> Masters, treat your slaves justly and fairly, knowing that you also have a Master in heaven.[33]

The key New Testament teaching is that God shows no partiality toward human beings:

> And Peter opened his mouth and said: "Truly I perceive that God shows no partiality."[34]

> For God shows no partiality.[35]

> Slaves, obey in everything those who are your earthly masters, not with eye service, as men-pleasers, but in singleness of heart, fearing the Lord. Whatever your task, work heartily, as serving the Lord and not men, knowing that from the Lord you will receive the inheritance as your reward; you are serving the Lord Christ. For the wrongdoer will be paid back for the wrong he has done and there is no partiality.[36]

> For as many of you as were baptized into Christ have put on Christ. There is neither Jew nor Greek, there is neither slave nor free, there is neither male nor female; for you are all one in Christ Jesus.[37]

The point of all these quotations is that "the ground is level at the foot of the Cross." Christians are all one in Christ Jesus. There is no partiality. We are all Abraham's offspring.[38] We are all brothers and sisters in the family of God, whether slave or free.

Therefore, Paul could write to Philemon, a slaveholder and Christian, about his runaway slave, Onesimus, who had become a Christian, saying, "I appeal to you for my child [in the faith], Onesimus, whose father I have become in my imprisonment."[39] Paul goes on to say,

> I am sending him back to you, sending my very heart. I would have been glad to keep him with me, in order that he might serve me on your behalf during my imprisonment for the gospel; but I preferred to do nothing without your consent in order that your goodness might not be by compulsion but of your own free will. Perhaps this is why he was parted from you for a while, that you might have him back forever, no longer as a slave, but more than a slave, as a beloved brother … both in the flesh and in the Lord.[40]

In this passage, Paul honors the civil laws of the day but, at the same time appeals to a higher law, a law of love and equality, which, in due course, would lead to a change in the culture and its laws.

It is clear that when one really understands that one's slave is one's brother in Christ, there is no more slavery. Nevertheless, neither Jesus nor any of the evangelists whose letters are found in the New Testament preached the social message of abolition. Their commission was to go "make disciples of all nations,"[41] not, "Go preach the abolition of slavery." Instead, they preached a Gospel that carried within it the seeds of the destruction of slavery.

THE HISTORY OF ABOLITION[42]

It was in 1754, one hundred years before the Civil War, that the American movement for the abolition of slavery began. Prior to that time, individuals – such as Samuel Sewall in 1700 – had written and published abolitionist tracts, but no organized group had yet begun an abolitionist movement.

The first movement against slavery began at the Philadelphia Yearly Meeting of the Quakers,[43] a Christian sect devoted to peace. At that 1754 meeting, a tract by John Woolman, "Some Considerations on the Keeping of Negroes," was approved for distribution to the whole assembly. Another tract, distributed the following year, contained the conclusion:

> Finally, brethren, we entreat you in … gospel love, seriously to weigh the cause of detaining them in bondage. If it be for your own private gain, or any motive other than their good, it is much to be feared that the love of God, and the influence of the Holy Spirit is not the prevailing principle in you.[44]

In 1758, the Yearly Meeting appointed a five-man committee to visit all Quaker slaveholders and, in the 1770s, Quaker Yearly Meetings throughout the Northeast prohibited members from owning slaves under penalty of exclusion.[45] It should come as no surprise that, in *Uncle Tom's Cabin*, Quakers are specifically mentioned as helping the runaways George, Eliza and Harry.

Two prominent framers of the Constitution, Benjamin Franklin and Benjamin Rush, both Quakers, headed their Society for the Promotion of the Abolition of Slavery in 1787.

At the time of the writing and ratification of the U.S. Constitution in the late 1770s, the issue of slavery had the potential to make the uniting of the colonies impossible. If slavery had been prohibited in the Constitution, there would have been no United States of America. The southern states would not have joined. In fact, the Constitution specifically prohibited

Congress from passing any law abolishing slavery until 1808, 20 years after the adoption of the Constitution.[46]

In 1790, though, the Quakers stepped forward with a proposal to the new Congress calling for an end to the slave trade.[47] It was signed by, among others, Benjamin Franklin – next to George Washington, himself, probably the most prestigious of the Founding Fathers – and so could not be ignored.[48] At the time of the Constitution's adoption there was an assumption by the northern states that the issue of slavery would be dealt with in due time, but the southern states had an entirely different perspective. Many northerners felt slavery to be an implicit contradiction in the American Republic that could not and would not last. Already, in 1776, the Continental Congress had voted to retain its prohibition on the importation of African slaves.[49] In the only book he ever published, Thomas Jefferson proposed a plan whereby all slaves born after 1800 would eventually become free.[50] But at the time of ratification it was believed that any ultimate resolution of the slavery issue would sink the Constitution entirely. Bound by the Constitution, Congress took no steps to adopt the Quaker proposal in 1790. For the time being, the issue of slavery was left to the states.

As for President George Washington, his sole aim was to institute and retain the Union. The slavery issue had to be secondary. And, of course, he himself was a slaveholder. But in his will he granted his slaves freedom, providing a comfortable living for the old and infirm slaves from that time until death and supporting the younger slaves until they reached adulthood. It was "a clear statement of his personal rejection of slavery."[51]

For their part, the states began making slavery illegal in their constitutions: Massachusetts, prior to the Union in 1771; Vermont in 1777; New Hampshire in 1779; Pennsylvania in 1780 and Rhode Island and Connecticut in 1784.[52] New York and New Jersey, with the largest slave populations in the North, did not follow immediately. Suffice it to say that slavery became the most prominent national issue in its first 70 years of existence until, in the Civil War, it was settled once and for all.

Soon, the anti-slavery movement involved far more than just Quakers. Prominent clergy in Harriet Beecher Stowe's family became involved. The American Anti-Slavery Movement was founded in 1833. By 1838, there were more than 1,000 local chapters with more than 300 "traveling" and "local" agents, the vast majority of whom were ordained clergy. The movement, therefore, spread primarily through local churches. The tracts of the Society were entirely Christian in their pitch, as illustrated by these quotations:

> [laws] admitting the right of slavery, are therefore, before God, utterly null and void … an audacious usurpation of divine perogative.[53]

> We plant ourselves upon the Declaration of Independence and the truths of Divine Revelation, as upon the Everlasting Rock.[54]

The Protestant churches demanded an end to slavery. The pope demanded an end to slavery.[55] In the end it was one man, William Wilberforce, a Christian member of British Parliament, who, by continual advocacy, brought about the first action to end slavery in the British Empire: the 1807 passage of a motion to abolish the slave trade.[56] The government of Britain then enforced this action by patrolling the African coast. Over the next 50 years, the British Navy seized 1,600 slave ships, freeing more than 150,000 slaves in transit. The effect of this was, of course, to end the African slave trade for all countries.

But existing slave populations still had to be dealt with. In 1833, one month after Wilberforce's death, British Parliament passed an action ending slavery in all British colonies and compensating planters (farmers) with an enormous sum, equal to one-half of the annual budget of Great Britain.[57]

The United States solved the problem once and for all in the crucible of the Civil War, which ended in 1865. Despite all other motives for the war, such as tariffs and state's rights, for the North, the war was a war about slavery. Before the Civil War had ended, one Union soldier had died for every 10 slaves set free. More than 600,000 Americans died in that war – more than in World War I or World War II. It was a war about moral vision nurtured by the Christian faith. In the end, slavery was abolished in Great Britain, the United States and throughout the Western world.

REVISIONIST HISTORY

Rodney Stark comments on this moral vision:

> The abolitionists knew that theirs was a religious movement, and so did several generations of historians. But during the latter half of the 20th century, many historians decided they knew better.[58]

What he is referring to is the fact that some recent historians have sought to claim that the moral arguments behind the abolitionist movement were a product of the "Enlightenment,"[59] not Christianity. Stark points out, on the contrary, "a virtual Who's Who of Enlightenment figures fully accepted slavery."[60] Thomas Hobbes, John Locke, Voltaire, Edmund Burke and David Hume openly sanctioned slavery and considered the abolitionist movements to be made up of religious fanatics.[61] Stark concludes:

> It was not philosophers or secular intellectuals who assembled the moral indictment of slavery, but the very people they held in such contempt: men and women having intense Christian faith, who opposed slavery because it was a sin.[62]

The gift of the abolition of slavery was a Christian gift to the West, which ultimately shamed most of the rest of the world into taking similar steps. It is a precious gift that raised the moral standards and economic possibilities of every nation it touched. Today, it is almost impossible for us to conceive what our lives would be like without it. After the recent election of Barack Obama as President, African American mothers are even able to say to their children, "You may one day even be the president of the United States."

CHAPTER FIVE

CHRISTIANITY AND THE EMANCIPATION OF WOMEN

T he great difficulty in the matter of the emancipation of women has always been the fact that there are physical and psychological differences between men and women. The case can and should be made that men and women are equal. But they are not identical.

Women bear children; men don't. They nurse babies; men don't. They have higher voices than men. They are, on average, both smaller and shorter than men. They tend to be physically weaker than men. But they also tend to live longer than men. It is almost embarrassing to have to point out these differences, but it must be done because there are people today who insist on androgyny: the belief that men and women are, apart from the inequities of social development, identical.

Beyond the obvious, it is clear that these differences have ramifications on male and female roles. Men run, carry, jump and fight better because they are bigger and stronger. That's why we have separate men's and women's sports, for example. It's also why women don't play in the NFL. And when superior male strength and size is considered alongside the whole childbearing process, demanding a woman's full focus from pregnancy through caring for the newborn, it is not surprising that, historically, men have assumed the role of protector and women the role of the protected.

This is why the cry on the Titanic was, "Women and children first!"

To enter still more controversial territory, there are psychological differences between men as a group and women as a group. There is a maternal instinct felt by women not felt in the same way by men. Women tend to be more sexually faithful than men. Women rarely rape men. Men and women mature differently. Men don't have PMS (premenstrual syndrome). There may even be subtle intellectual differences between the two sexes. Equal, but not identical.

So where did this idea of "equal" come from? Taliban officials certainly did not consider the women they beat on the streets of Afghanistan their equals. Hindu men have never had to throw themselves on the funeral pyres of their wives as women did for their husbands. Husbands in India who kill their wives because their dowries are not large enough don't consider them to be their equals.

In the Third World, female enrollment in primary education is 65 percent that of males; in secondary education it drops to 37 percent. Two-thirds of the world's illiterates are women. How does that correspond with the general thought that men and women are equal? It doesn't!

In China and India, the vast preponderance of abortions involve female babies. In Islam, male martyrs who sacrifice their lives in *jihad* are promised multiple virgins when they enter paradise, according to the Koran, but the Koran is entirely silent about similar rewards for female martyrs.

In Greece and Rome, men greatly outnumbered women because exposure (to be left outside without warmth or milk) of female infants was "legal, morally accepted, and widely practiced by all social classes in the Greco-Roman world."[1] In a study of 600 families at Delphi, only six had raised more than one daughter.[2] In a letter written in 1 B.C. to his pregnant wife, one Hilarion said,

> Know that I am still in Alexandria. And do not worry if they all come back and I remain in Alexandria. I ask and beg you to take good care of our baby son. ... If you are delivered of a child [before I come home], if it is a boy, keep it, if a girl, discard it.[3]

Men and women clearly were not valued equally.

In fact, just as slavery has been practiced throughout history by every culture that could afford it, so the inequality of men and women has been practiced throughout history by all cultures. Even in Judaism the prayer, "I thank thee, O Lord, that I was not born a slave or a Gentile or a woman,"[4] was prayed daily by male Jews. So where did the idea of male-female equality come from?

It came from the Christian faith. It is a great idea of the Christian faith that *men and women are created equal.*

THE OLD TESTAMENT BASIS

The first chapter of Genesis draws no distinction between men and women and, thus, announces this equality:

> So God created man in His own image, in the image of God He
> created him: male and female He created them. And God blessed
> them and said to them, "Be fruitful and multiply, and fill the earth
> and subdue it; and have dominion over the fish of the sea and over
> the birds of the air and over every living thing that moves upon
> the earth."[5]

The word "man" here is clearly generic, meant to include women – "male and female He created them." Women are equally the bearers of God's image, equally commanded to be fruitful and multiply, equally given the task of filling the earth and subduing it, equally given dominion over creation.[6]

The author of the New Testament letter to the Hebrews reviews Old Testament history in chapter 11 and singles out two women for commendation: Sarah and Rahab. To this list could be added Deborah, Ruth, Naomi and Esther. In a world in which so many contemporary cultures devalued women – including, at times, the Jewish culture of New Testament times – the Hebrew Scriptures were noteworthy for the prominence given to many women.

THE NEW TESTAMENT BASIS

In the New Testament, women were fully a part of the ministry of Jesus and the community of believers.

First of all, women were a regular, recognized part of Jesus' traveling entourage. At the Cross, three women are mentioned as among those "who, when He was in Galilee, followed Him and ministered to Him," and then Mark adds: "and also many other women who came up with Him to Jerusalem."[7] Moreover, two women went with Joseph of Arimathea and his servants to put Jesus into the tomb.[8] After the Sabbath, early on the morning of the first day of the week, it was again women who went to the tomb to anoint the body of Jesus[9] and, therefore, women who first heard the news of His resurrection.[10] When they told the disciples, this seemed "an idle tale and they did not believe them."[11] To understand that, one must know that in Jewish culture women were ordinarily disparaged as witnesses and in law were specifically disqualified as reliable witnesses of anything.

According to the Gospel of John, when Mary Magdalene found the tomb empty, she told Peter and John. They then went to the tomb themselves but left immediately upon seeing that what she said was true. It was to Mary, who lingered at the tomb weeping, that Jesus made His first post-resurrection appearance.[12]

The weight of this fact is lost upon those of us who have a very different attitude toward women because we live in the Christian West. To the Jews of the time, for a woman to be the first witness would have been a colossal joke. In fact, it may have been in deference to the low place of women in the Mediterranean cultures that Paul failed to mention Mary Magdalene as the first witness in his catalogue of Resurrection witnesses (I Corinthians 15:4, 5).

Jesus spent a good portion of His ministry befriending women, speaking to women, healing women, praising their faith and, in general, elevating them above the inequality assigned them by their culture. Moreover, He made it quite clear in His answer to the Sadducees' question about the woman who was widowed seven times that, "in the resurrection they neither marry nor are given in marriage, but are like angels in heaven."[13] In other words, in heaven, distinctions between men and women disappear.

Christians look forward to a heaven in which even the differences of roles in marriage and married life are left behind, anticipating an equality quite unlike any found in other religions of the world. And since Christians in the New Testament were always aware of their heavenly citizenship with "one foot in the grave and the other on a banana peel," this anticipation could not have been anything less than transformational in their gender attitudes here and now.

All this must be considered against the background of repeated New Testament teachings about a difference in male and female marital roles, primarily that the wife is to submit to the leadership of the husband.[14] Peter tells husbands that they must "live considerately" with their wives, "bestowing honor on the woman as the weaker sex." Why? Because, he says, "you are joint heirs of the grace of life."[15] In other words, the equality of heaven was clearly to be on the minds of those New Testament husbands. Paul, for his part, spends three verses in Ephesians 5 telling wives they should "be subject" to their husbands' leadership, and then spends the next nine verses telling husbands they should love their wives even to the point of sacrificing their lives for them.[16] In other words, if there is an inequality of roles here, it is the husbands who are given the tougher row to hoe.

To sum up the issue of equality in the New Testament, Paul clearly says in Galatians 3:27, 28:

> For as many of you as were baptized into Christ have put on
> Christ, there is neither Jew nor Greek, there is neither slave nor
> free, there is neither male nor female; for you are all one in Christ
> Jesus.

And so we find women in the New Testament teaching,[17] serving as deacons,[18] "risking their necks" for Paul,[19] prophesying[20] (the greatest of the spiritual gifts)[21] and "laboring side by side [with Paul] in the gospel."[22] No second-class status here.[23] Further, women are not excluded from any of the "spiritual gifts" in the passages that discuss them.[24]

One church historian[25] makes a strong case for the fact that the early Christian Church had a larger proportion of women than men in a culture in which men outnumbered women, composing 58 percent of the population.[26] The reasons for this are manifold,[27] but chief among them are that the Christian Church practiced neither infanticide nor abortion, as was true in surrounding cultures. Infanticide tended to deplete the number of female babies and abortion the number of female adults, since abortion often resulted in the death of the mother. It should come as no surprise, therefore, that the Christian faith was especially attractive to women and, in the New Testament, women of higher rank tended to become Christians before their husbands. Unlike Christianity's chief religious rival in Roman culture, Mithraism – which was a male-only religion[28] – Christianity welcomed women as equals.

EMANCIPATION IN AMERICA

With its basic openness toward women, it is not surprising that Christianity became the primary source of ideas that produced the emancipation of women in America. As enshrined in the Declaration of Independence, using the term "men" generically, our founders declared:

> We hold these truths to be self-evident that all men are created
> equal, that they are endowed by their Creator with certain
> unalienable Rights, that among these are Life, Liberty and the
> pursuit of happiness.

In the early days of America, there was so much need for women in the home that there was little discussion of issues of equality. The women cooked and washed, spun cloth and made clothing, tended fires and split wood, tended vegetable gardens, fed animals and assisted in farming. And, of course, they bore, raised and educated the children. Also, in the early days, only property holders could vote, and husbands were the owners of record, so women did not vote.[29]

As with abolition, American Quakers were among the early leaders on this issue. In a circular letter dated 1675, a group of Quaker women wrote to other Quaker women,

> In the blessed unity of the Spirit of grace our Souls Salute you
> who are sanctified in Christ Jesus, and called to be Saints, who
> are of the true and Royal offspring of Christ Jesus ... for as many
> of us as are baptized into Christ, have put on Christ; for we are
> all children of God by faith in Christ Jesus, where there is neither
> male nor female etc. but are all one [in] Christ Jesus.[30]

The body of the letter encouraged the continuance of customary monthly meetings of women in each Quaker meeting in which minutes were kept, collections received and mission projects supported. Quaker women were well organized, with local monthly meetings and yearly regional meetings.

At the time of the American Revolution, the issue of the absurdity of women's inability to vote was raised by such men of rank as John Adams.[31] On March 31, 1776, his wife Abigail wrote to him:

> I long to hear that you have declared [independence] – and by
> the way in the new Code of Laws which I suppose it will be
> necessary for you to make, I desire you would Remember the
> Ladies, and be more generous and favorable to them than your
> ancestors. Do not put such unlimited power in the hands of the
> Husbands. Remember all men would be tyrants if they could.
> If particular care and attention is not paid to the Ladies we are
> determined to foment a Rebellion, and will not hold ourselves
> bound by any laws in which we have no voice or representation.
> ... Men of Sense in all Ages abhor those customs which treat us

only as the Vassals of your Sex. Regard us then as Beings placed
by Providence under your protection and in imitation of the
Supreme Being make use of that power only for our happiness.[32]

John Adams' tongue-in-cheek reply said,

You know we [husbands] are the subjects. We have only the Name
of Masters, and rather than give up this, which would completely
subject us to the Despotism of the Petticoat, I hope General
Washington, and all our brave heroes would fight.[33]

But Abigail had made her point: when a new country with laws of its
own was formed, the role of women should not be neglected.

As men thought about the role of women in society many, such as
Benjamin Rush, realized the need for women's education. In a letter dated
1787, Rush wrote to the principal of a women's academy to express these
thoughts:

The female members of the community ... must be the stewards
and guardians of their husband's property. That education,
therefore, will be most proper for our women which teaches them
to discharge the duties of those offices with the most success
and reputation. ... The instruction of children naturally devolves
upon the women. It becomes us ... to prepare these by a suitable
education, for the discharge of this most important duty of
mothers.

To this he added that they should be able to teach "the principles of
liberty and government," to speak and spell correctly, to know "figures
and bookkeeping," to be acquainted with "geography, history, biography
and travels," to be acquainted with "the first principles of astronomy and
natural philosophy" and there was more, too much to cite.

Suffice it to say that the education of women was on the minds of
many Founding Fathers and, by 1837, the first women's college, Mount
Holyoke, was founded. In 1835, Mary Lyon made a speech to raise money
to establish Mount Holyoke:

After much deliberation, prayer, and correspondence, the friends
of the Redeemer have determined to erect a school for the
daughters of the church, the object of which shall be to fit them
for the highest degree of usefulness. ... The seminary [an old
term for a women's college] is to be entirely based on Christian
principles; and while it is to be furnished with teachers of the

> highest character and experience, and to have every advantage
> which the state of female education in this country will allow,
> its brightest feature will be, that it is a school for Christ. ... It
> is designed to cultivate the missionary spirit among its pupils;
> the feeling that they should live for God, and do something as
> teachers or in such other ways as Providence may direct.

It is hard to imagine a more explicit Christian basis and purpose.

Forty years later, in 1875, the second women's college, Wellesley, was founded by Henry and Pauline Durant, ardent evangelical Christians. In 1880, Noah Porter, president of Yale, spoke at Wellesley on the theme, "The Christian College," a manifesto that later circulated as a pamphlet. The occasion was the laying of the cornerstone of the second building. The Rev. S. F. Smith wrote a hymn for the occasion, "Founded on Christ."

By 1828, Dwight L. Moody had joined Wellesley's board of trustees. Each member of the board and each professor – all women – were required to be members of an evangelical church. In its first announcement, the college proclaimed, "This institution will be Christian in its influence, discipline, and course of instruction." Again, we find that secular forces were not the first to advance college education for women, but Christian.[34]

At about the same time, Vassar and Smith were founded with explicitly Christian emphases. Similar purposes also accompanied the foundings of Cornell and Oberlin, the first co-educational colleges in America.[35]

In this same period the American women's rights movement began. Its beginning was officially marked by a "Declaration of Sentiments" that emerged from a women's convention in Seneca Falls, New York, in 1848. The convention was organized by five Christian women: four Quaker and one Presbyterian. The declaration began,

> When, in the course of human events, it becomes necessary for
> one portion of the family of man to assume among the people of
> the earth a position different from that which they have hitherto
> occupied, but one to which the laws of nature and of nature's God
> entitle them, a decent respect to the opinions of mankind requires
> that they should declare the causes that impel them to such a
> course.[36]

The declaration went on to advocate for "the elective franchise," that is, the right to vote; "representation in the halls of legislation;" property rights; changes in the equality of divorce laws; access to college education; and more.

The 14th Amendment's passage in 1865 gave the right to vote to freed slaves and was worded in such a way as to give the right to vote to every *male* citizen over 21 years of age – for the first time explicitly identifying the right of suffrage with the male gender. The issue of women's suffrage, then, dominated the period from 1866-1920. It was in 1920, with the passage of the 19th Amendment to the Constitution, that women were finally given the right to vote.

CONCLUSION

The road to women's suffrage was paved by opening college education to women, which had begun through the efforts of Christians more than 80 years earlier. By 1910, 8,000 women had graduated from American colleges.

Though a long time coming, that great turning point in the emancipation of women represented by giving women the vote was accomplished by building on a Biblical foundation established long before America was even discovered – the great idea that men and women are created equal.

CHAPTER SIX

CHRISTIANITY AND
AMERICAN DEMOCRACY

In the last month of 2004, an article appeared in *The New York Times* headlined, "God, American History, and a Fifth-Grade Class."[1] It described the troubles of a public school teacher in Cupertino, California, who brought up the subject of God in his lessons on colonial history.

The ruckus began when the teacher used a handout of President George W. Bush's proclamation for the National Day of Prayer as an example of a presidential proclamation. A parent complained that doing so amounted to "too much religion in the classroom."

This was not the first time the teacher had been known to reference Christianity in his teaching of colonial history. So, his principal called him into her office and told him that all future handouts would have to be screened by her for "inappropriate religious content." Previously, a handout with excerpts from the Declaration of Independence had aroused the ire of parents for its mention of "Nature's God," the words "created" and "sacred" and the phrases "endowed by their Creator" and "divine Providence" – all original text of the Declaration of Independence. The parents of Cupertino were actually objecting to the wording of one of America's founding documents!

The problem, of course, is that if Christianity cannot be referenced in a course on colonial history and the founding of America, then the course cannot be taught at all. To leave out such references would, in fact, be to rewrite history and, thus, to teach a history that wasn't, a history that didn't happen. It would be like teaching the history of baseball without mentioning Jackie Robinson or the history of science without mentioning Einstein – because of a prejudice against African Americans or Jews. Even so, a prejudice against Christianity in writing (or rewriting) the history of this country would be so significant as to make the end product impossibly skewed and divorced from reality.

One of the best illustrations of the long-term influence of great ideas is the influence of the Christian faith in the shaping of American democracy. That influence made itself felt in a variety of ways – in American morals, industry and optimism, to name a few – but the great idea of the Christian faith at the core of its influence on American democracy is the claim that *every human being is a sinner; every human being is loved by God.*

As Glen Tinder points out, beginning with the very first sentence of his great book, *The Political Meaning of Christianity,*

> "God so loved the world," according to the Gospel of John, "that He gave His only Son, that whoever believes in Him should not perish but have eternal life." This short sentence summarizes the Christian faith: God has come to human beings, creatures alienated from the source and end of their lives and existing therefore in need and desperation, and has transformed their situation. In the mystery of Christ's crucifixion and resurrection, all of the guilt and hatred dividing human beings from God and from one another has been overcome ... in consequence, every person is exalted.[2]

To use Tinder's phrase, "every person is exalted," is not to say, of course, that every person is a Christian. John specifically says that only those who "believe" are. But it is to say that every person is loved by God and, therefore, "exalted." The Christian faith is a kind of Cinderella story or, in more modern terms, a *Shrek* story. We all are pursued by a transforming love, the seeking, forgiving love of God and, therefore, we are "exalted." That love makes every human being of inestimable value. Every man, woman or child who has ever lived in this world is loved by God. Every human being is dear to God, however sinful he or she may be. As Paul says, "But God shows His love for us in that while we were yet sinners, Christ died for us."[3]

The Christian faith is a bad news/good news Gospel. We are all sinners. (Can anyone doubt that looking around the world in any period of history?) But God loves us anyway. And He wants to transform us, if only we will turn back to Him through the road or "way" that He has opened in Jesus, the Son of God and Savior of the world. The Gospel is reality – this is an evil world. And it is hope – God loves and seeks us.

This completely changes the way in which we see ourselves and others. No one has a heart of gold, but everyone has a value beyond reckoning. American democracy is based on these two great Christian facts. The checks and balances in our political structure come from the first – the fact that every human being is a sinner. Our understanding of human dignity comes from the second – the fact that every human being is loved by God.

TWO REVOLUTIONS

Two revolutions occurred within 20 years of each other: the American Revolution in 1776 and the French Revolution in 1792. The American Revolution was based on the perspective of the Christian faith, and the French Revolution was based on the perspective of secularism. The two could not have been more different.

In America, the Declaration of Independence was adopted by the action of the Second Continental Congress on July 4, 1776, as the unanimous declaration of the 13 colonies. After the Revolutionary War had won that independence, many of the same individuals met again in 1787 to draft a plan for the governing of the new nation. That plan was the Constitution of the United States. Two years later, after ratification in 1789, the new government began to operate.

The Declaration of Independence and the Constitution are two separate documents whose adoption was separated by 13 years, but together they form America's foundation. In the first, the founders set forth their moral vision and the type of government it implied. In the second, that government was established in detail. Finally, two years later, the Bill of Rights (the first 10 amendments), suggested by various states in the ratification process of the Constitution, was added. Thus America's founding documents are the Declaration of Independence and the Constitution, as initially amended.

The Declaration of Independence, written primarily by Thomas Jefferson, made it plain that the rights upon which the nation was to be founded were rights granted by God. The second paragraph begins with these words.

> We hold these Truths to be self-evident, that all Men are created
> equal, that they are endowed by their Creator with certain
> unalienable Rights.

The basis, therefore, upon which this nation was founded was an understanding about the nature of human beings as created by God – and, specifically, in the cultural context at the founding, the God of the Bible.

In France, on the other hand, the basis upon which the nation was founded was reason – and, specifically, reason within a secular state devoid of any remnant of religion.[4] In France, the revolution was not a war against a foreign power, but a war against the Catholic Church and its place in the nation's former understanding of itself. Some participants in the French Revolution proposed that Notre Dame Cathedral be reconsecrated as the "Temple of Reason."[5] As one author describes the situation,

> The National Assembly passed a resolution deliberately declaring
> "There is no God;" vacated the throne of Deity by simple
> resolution, abolished the Sabbath, unfrocked her ministers of
> religion, turned temples of spiritual worship into places of secular
> business, and enthroned a vile woman as the Goddess of Reason.[6]

In Paris, the Goddess of Reason mentioned was actually personified by an actress who was carried into the cathedral by men dressed as Romans.[7] The popular Convention on October 5, 1793, voted "to abolish the Christian Calendar and introduce a republican calendar," establishing September 22, 1792, as the beginning of Year One of the new era.[8]

The American Revolution embraced Christianity for its core principles. The French Revolution rejected all religious precepts.

ALEXIS DE TOCQUEVILLE

The French Revolution culminated in a bloodbath of executions induced by revolutionary fever. So much was this true that the French sociologist, Alexis de Tocqueville, in his book *Democracy in America*, written in the early 1800s, warned against tyrannical republics and commented on the contemporary situation in his native France:

> It is not a question now of finding out whether we are to have
> a monarchy or a republic in France: but we still want to know

whether it will be an agitated or tranquil republic, an orderly or
disorderly republic, pacific or warlike, liberal or oppressive, a
republic which threatens the sacred rights of property and of the
family, or one which recognizes and honors them.[9]

It was a revolution without a moral anchor.

In fact, one of the chief distinctions of the American Republic, in the
estimation of de Tocqueville, was its Christian foundations. He wrote,

The religious atmosphere of the country was the first thing that
struck me on arrival in the United States. The longer I stayed
in the country, the more conscious I became of the important
political consequences resulting from this novel situation. In
France I had seen the spirits of religion and freedom almost
always marching in opposite directions. In America I found them
intimately linked together. ... My longing to understand this
phenomenon increased daily.[10]

He wrote of stopping at the home of a rich planter in "one of the
remotest parts of Pennsylvania." It turned out that his host was French,
too. As they sat by the fireside, his host talked about property rights, about
the hierarchy that wealth establishes, about obeying the law and then about
the support of order and freedom provided by religious ideas, that is,
Christianity. Finally, his host inadvertently quoted the authority of Jesus
Christ in support of one of his political opinions. That conversation could
never have occurred in France. The opinions expressed by the host were
as far from France, politically and spiritually, as were the two Frenchmen
who sat by the fire talking that night, geographically. But it could take
place in America, a land where Christian influence prevailed.[11]

De Tocqueville divided his comments on the influence of Christianity
in America into two categories: direct influence and indirect influence.[12]
Regarding direct influence he said,

Most of English America was peopled by men who ... brought to
the New World a Christianity which ... favored the establishment
of a temporal republic and democracy.[13]

Regarding indirect influence, he said the effect is "much greater."
De Tocqueville said that all Christian sects in America preach the same
morality in the name of God:

America is still the place where the Christian religion has
kept the greatest real power over men's souls – and nothing

better demonstrates how useful and natural it is to man, since the country where it now has widest sway is both the most enlightened and the freest.[14]

He continued,

For the Americans the ideas of Christianity and liberty are so completely mingled that it is almost impossible to get them to conceive of the one without the other.[15]

EARLY SETTLEMENTS

The early settling of America was a saga of trial and failure. In 1562, a group of French Huguenots seeking haven from religious persecution arrived in Florida, then traveled to South Carolina. St. Augustine, where they first arrived, still claims to be the earliest continuous settlement in the United States. In 1585, a group of ships came from England to settle Roanoke Island, off the coast of North Carolina, but the settlement soon disappeared without a trace. In 1607, the settlement at Jamestown, Virginia, began, but the Jamestown expedition was not a settlement of families. It was a group of gentlemen adventurers plagued by misfortune. During its first 20 years, it almost ceased to exist more than once, in spite of continual new arrivals by ship from England.[16]

The first genuine settlement of families in America is generally acknowledged to be that of the Pilgrims, who came over on the *Mayflower* and settled at Plymouth, Massachusetts, in late 1620. The first 30 years of the history of that settlement were meticulously chronicled by Governor William Bradford and published under the title, *Of Plymouth Plantation: Bradford's History of the Plymouth Settlement.*[17] The Plymouth Pilgrims have always been larger than life in American history, and their Christian faith, character and motivations have become the principle legend of our founding.

The Pilgrims were devout English Christians who came to America for many reasons. In listing them, Bradford concludes with these words,

Last and not least, they cherished a great hope and inward zeal of laying good foundations ... for the propagation and advance of the Gospel of Jesus Christ in the remote parts of the world.[18]

Put simply, they saw themselves as missionaries to the American Indians. Their journey began with a day-long prayer meeting.[19] Arriving at

Plymouth in November of 1620, half of their small number of 100 settlers died that first winter.[20] At times, there were only six or seven healthy settlers to attend to the needs of the sick and dying. Nevertheless, the record of Bradford is filled with Scripture, prayer and thanksgiving for the providential surprises that, again and again, they received from God.

Other settlements quickly followed: one in Connecticut in 1638, another led by a Quaker, William Penn, in Pennsylvania (1701). All were founded on the precepts of Christianity by people who professed "to believe in Jesus Christ, the Savior of the world."[21]

COLONIAL PERIOD STATE CONSTITUTIONS

The first constitutions of the colonial period were state constitutions. Under the national Constitution, adopted in 1789, powers not delegated to the national government remained with the states.[22] As originally conceived, one of those areas of states' rights was the matter of religion. The First Amendment in the Bill of Rights makes that division of powers doubly clear by saying, in part:

> Congress shall make no law respecting an establishment of
> religion or prohibiting the free exercise thereof. ...

The whole matter of religion, then, was left to the states.

Thus, the Delaware constitution, for example, "established" the Christian religion by proclaiming the state "Christian," while not establishing a specific sect or denomination. Clergymen were prohibited from holding office while acting as pastors. The Delaware constitution also stated:

> Every person who shall be chosen a member of either house, or
> appointed to any office or place of trust shall ... also make and
> subscribe the following declaration, to wit: "I do profess faith in
> God the Father, and in Jesus Christ His only Son, and in the Holy
> Ghost, one God blessed for evermore; and I do acknowledge the
> Holy Scriptures of the Old and New Testaments to be given by
> divine inspiration."[23]

The New Jersey Constitution of 1776 put the matter of religious establishment negatively by saying:

> No protestant inhabitant of this colony shall be denied the
> enjoyment of any civil right merely on account of his religious

principles; but all persons, professing belief in the faith of a
Protestant sect ... shall be capable of being elected into any
office of profit or trust, or being a member of either branch of the
legislature.

Protestantism was both established and protected from ever being
disestablished. The original constitution of 1683 protected religious liberty,
required every civil magistrate to affirm and swear a binding oath to Jesus
Christ and explicitly exempted atheism from such protection of liberty.[24]

In Georgia, the 1777 constitution protected liberty of conscience
but mandated that legislative representatives "shall be of the Protestant
religion."[25]

Maryland's constitution of 1776, as a colony settled by English
Catholics, simply said,

All persons, professing the Christian religion are equally entitled
to protection in their religious liberty.[26]

Though not going so far as to establish Roman Catholicism, it
nevertheless was understood that all citizens would at least be Christians.

Massachusetts' constitution of 1780 stated,

It is the right as well as the duty of all men in society, publicly,
and at stated seasons to worship the SUPREME BEING, the great
Creator and Preserver of the universe.

And,

No person shall be eligible [for office] unless ... he shall declare
himself to be of the Christian religion.[27]

The New Hampshire constitution of 1784 stated,

Every individual has a natural and unalienable right to worship
GOD according to the dictates of his own conscience, and reason;
and no subject shall be hurt, molested, or restrained in his person,
liberty or estate for worshiping GOD in the manner and season
most agreeable to the dictates of his own conscience, or for his
religious profession, sentiments or persuasion; provided he doth
not disturb the public peace, or disturb others, in their religious
worship.

Nevertheless, state office holders were required to be of the "protestant
religion."[28]

The 1776 constitution of North Carolina said that all men have "a natural and unalienable right to worship God according to the dictates of their own conscience." Nevertheless,

> No person who shall deny the being of God, or the truth of the Protestant religion, or the divine authority of the Old and New Testaments, or who shall hold religious principles incompatible with the freedom and safety of the State, shall be capable of holding any office or place of trust or profit in the civil department within the State.

This provision remained in effect until 1876.[29]

In Pennsylvania, the constitution of 1776 required that every member of the legislature should subscribe to the following:

> I do believe in one God, the Creator and Governor of the universe, the Rewarder of the good and the punisher of the wicked; and I acknowledge the Scriptures of the Old and New Testaments to be given by Divine Inspiration.

The 1790 Pennsylvania constitution reaffirms the foregoing and adds,

> No person who acknowledges the being of God, and a future state of rewards and punishments, shall, on account of his religious sentiments, be disqualified to hold any office or place of trust or profit under this commonwealth.[30]

These examples have been cited at length in order to describe the general religious tenor of all of the state constitutions before, during and after the adoption of the United States Constitution. They form such an incredible patchwork of different nuances of Christian perspective that it is understandable that the First Amendment was suggested and passed by all the states. They did not want the federal government to interfere in this well-established area of their common life.

The fact is, all these state constitutions contain some form of establishment of the Christian religion, yet all are different. Is it any wonder that the whole issue of establishment and of the particular wording of religious tests would be left to the states? No delegate to the constitutional convention of 1787 would want to fiddle with that because the delegate would be bound to alienate some state or other and because there was no need – there was already so much essential agreement among the states. The agreement was simply, by cultural consensus rather than national law, that this was a Christian society and that no specific sect or denomination should ever be made into an established national church.

Yet this great fact is little understood today – the framers of the constitution always understood this to be a Christian society, but they never wanted any one church to be established by the national government. Their expectations of a Christian society are far from the broad expectations of a secular society found in the country today.

SEPARATION OF CHURCH AND STATE

Many people today are not only unaware that the phrase "separation of church and state" does not occur in the Constitution,[31] but they also have no understanding of how strongly the founders believed this to be a nation specifically founded on Christian understandings and principles. How many Americans today, for example, are aware that religious tests for state officeholders were common and widely supported at the time of the Constitution's writing – and that the Constitution itself did nothing to undermine or negate them?

The origin of the phrase "separation of church and state" is found in a letter from Thomas Jefferson, responding to an 1802 letter from the Danbury Baptist Association. The association wrote to him to express its concern over a rumor that a particular denomination was soon to be recognized as the national denomination. In his response, Jefferson said,

> I contemplate with solemn reverence that act of the whole
> American people which declared that their legislature should
> "make no law respecting an establishment of religion, or
> prohibiting the free exercise thereof," thus building a wall of
> separation between church and state.[32]

He meant that the national government was never going to establish any national denomination because the First Amendment, which he quoted to them, protected all churches from the interference of the federal government. It was, in other words, a one-directional wall protecting the "church" from interference on the part of the "state"[33] – that is, the national government. It is ironic that today the "separation of church and state" is commonly used to mean a wall protecting the *government* from any influence of the church.

That this was Jefferson's understanding of the phrase "separation of church and state" is evidenced further in an 1808 letter he wrote to Samuel Miller:

> I consider the government of the United States as interdicted by
> the Constitution from intermeddling with religious institutions.
> ... This results not only from the provision that no law shall be
> made respecting the establishment or free exercise of religion,
> but from that also which reserves to the States the powers not
> delegated to the United States.[34]

It can be argued, of course, that Christianity should not be imposed by state law any more than by national law. In citing these early state constitutions, I do not offer them as models for today. God desires free and voluntary worship, not that which is required by the dictates of a government. But these early constitutions do reflect a historical fact: The United States was founded with the expectation that its culture, its civil society, be Christian in character. Private religious principle would sustain the public morality that was believed essential to self-government.

To be clear, it was not the intention of the founders that the United States be a theocracy – no national government would impose religious beliefs and practices by force of law. Nor was the church to have civil power or authority delegated to it over secular matters. Thus, the power of the state and the power of the church were to be kept in separate realms.

But there is a great difference between separating the authority of the church from the authority of civil government and separating religious influence from public policy. The founders never intended the latter. Indeed, it was expected that a moral population sustained by religious principle would preserve civil government and their beneficial moral influence would be felt in public life and policy. Nevertheless, confusion reigns today because of an out-of-context and misunderstood phrase, "separation of church and state."

CHRISTIAN COUNTRY

One of the most interesting evidences of the fact that the United States, at the time of the Constitution's adoption and over the next 165 years, considered itself Christian in character is found in a multitude of Supreme Court decisions. The following are some quotations from some of those decisions.[35]

Vidal v. Girard's Executors (1844):

> Christianity ... is not to be maliciously and openly reviled. ... It
> is unnecessary for us ... to consider the establishment of a college

for the propagation of Deism, or any other form of infidelity.
Such a case is not to be presumed to exist in a Christian country.[36]

Murphy v. Ramsey and Othmes (1885) (A polygamy case and a decision protecting the family as a "holy" estate according to Biblical morality):

> No legislation ... [is] more necessary in the founding of a free
> and self-governing commonwealth ... than that which seeks to
> establish it on the basis of the idea of the family as consisting in
> ... the union for life of one woman and one man in the holy estate
> of matrimony.[37]

Davis v. Beason (1889) (This case involved bigamy and polygamy among Mormons in the western territories):

> Bigamy and polygamy are crimes by the laws of all civilized and
> Christian countries.[38]

Church of Holy Trinity v. United States (1892):

> No purpose of action against religion can be imputed to any
> legislation, state or national, because this is a religious people. ...
> This is a Christian nation.[39]

Even after the *Everson v. Board of Education* decision in 1947 the courts still affirmed in *Zorach v. Clauson* (1952):

> The First Amendment, however, does not say that in every and
> all respects there shall be a separation of church and state. ... We
> are a religious people whose institutions presuppose a supreme
> being.[40]

In the same vein, the following quotations are from Founding Fathers on the theme of the United States as a Christian nation.
John Jay, first chief justice of the U.S. Supreme Court:

> "Providence has given to our people the choice of their rulers,
> and it is the duty as well as privilege and interest of a Christian
> nation to ... prefer Christians for their rulers."[41]

Joseph Story, appointed to the Supreme Court by James Madison, serving for 34 years:

> "We are not to attribute [the First Amendment] to an indifference
> to religion in general, and especially to Christianity (which
> none could hold in more reverence than did the framers of the

Constitution) ... the universal sentiment in America was, that
Christianity ought to receive encouragement from the State."[42]

John Adams, second president of the United States:

> "We have no government armed with power capable of
> contending with human passions unbridled by morality and
> religion. Avarice, ambition, revenge, or gallantry would break the
> strongest cords of our Constitution as a whale goes through a net.
> Our Constitution was made only for a moral and religious people.
> It is wholly inadequate to the government of any other."[43]

Noah Webster, Revolutionary War soldier, one of the first Founding
Fathers to call for a constitutional convention and the author of the
dictionary bearing his name:

> "The religion which has introduced civil liberty, is the religion
> of Christ and His apostles, which enjoins humility, piety, and
> benevolence; which acknowledges in every person, a brother, or a
> sister, and citizen with equal rights. This is genuine Christianity,
> and to this we owe our free constitutions of government."[44]

SUPREME COURT CHANGES

In the case of *Everson v. Board of Education* (1947), the Supreme Court
did an abrupt about face. In general, the phrase "separation of church and
state' would no longer imply what Jefferson meant – that is, protection of
the churches from the interference of the national government – but, rather,
"separation of church and state" now meant protection of the national
government from the interference of Christianity.

In *Everson*, the court decided that the national government could
limit the "free exercise" of religion, thus eroding the First Amendment.[45]
At the same time, it also eroded the Tenth Amendment ("The powers not
delegated to the United States by the Constitution, nor prohibited by it to
the States, are reserved to the States respectively, or to the people") by
deciding that issues relating to religion would no longer be left primarily
to the states alone but would, instead, be assumed to be the province of
the national government. It did so by use of the due process clause of the
14th Amendment, adopted almost 90 years before (1868). (Amendments
13, 14 and 15 were the Civil War-era amendments that freed the slaves,
made them citizens and gave freed male slaves the right to vote.) The 14th

Amendment said, in part:

> No State shall make or enforce any law which shall abridge the
> privileges and indemnities of the citizens of the United States;
> nor shall any State deprive any person of life, liberty, or property,
> without due process of law; nor deny to any person within its
> jurisdiction the equal protection of the laws.[46]

Thus, nearly 90 years after the 14th Amendment was adopted, the U.S. Supreme Court used it to decide that the phrase "separation of church and state," which was not part of the Constitution anyway, meant the separation of basic religious principles from government. Specifically, in *Everson,* the court said:

> Neither a state nor the Federal Government ... can pass laws
> which aid one religion, aid all religions, or prefer one religion
> over another.[47]

In effect, *Everson* meant that the government was not only prohibited from preferring one denomination over another, it also prohibited a government preference for religion, in general. Government was now required to prefer irreligion over religion. This has resulted in government hostility toward religion in general. It establishes a "religion" of secularism. If intent counts for anything in the interpretation of the Constitution, as well it should, there is no question but that the Founding Fathers would have considered *Everson* a disaster.

To illustrate how deeply the court's animus against Christianity has become, Congress had to pass the Equal Access Bill of 1984 in order to guarantee student religious groups the same access to school facilities (after school) as was already extended to non-religious student groups. At the time, President Ronald Reagan commented,

> We even had to pass a law ... to allow student prayer groups the
> same access to school rooms after classes that a Young Marxist
> Society, for example, would already enjoy with no opposition.[48]

By 1987, four courts of appeals had ruled the equal access law unconstitutional, violating the Establishment Clause of the First Amendment. Finally, in 1990, the U.S. Supreme Court held that "Christian students did indeed have equal rights and deserved equal access to school activities and facilities."[49] It then took another six years for the Supreme Court to end the standoff with Congress and actually allow equal access.

Nevertheless, in *Everson,* a radical change had taken place that could not be remedied. History began to be rewritten in an effort to avoid the role of Christianity in the country's founding. In his book, *Censorship: Evidence of Bias in our Children's Textbooks,*[50] Paul Vitz published the results of a 1986 study. He found that Christianity had been written out of American social studies textbooks:

> In the first part of the project a total of sixty representative
> social studies textbooks were carefully evaluated … none of the
> books … contain one word referring to any religious activity in
> contemporary American life.[51]

It has been written out of public school readers and history texts, as well. Paul Vitz, for example, describes an incident between the author of a short story and the textbook publisher who wanted to reprint it:

> The issue centered on a children's story of hers called "Molly's
> Pilgrim." A major textbook publisher, Harcourt, Brace,
> Jovanovich, wanted to reprint part of the story for their third
> grade reader. But … the publishers wanted … to rewrite parts
> to make it more acceptable. They phoned [the author] and asked
> for her permission to reprint their modified version. [The author]
> refused. … They argued…, "If we mention God, some atheist
> will object. If we mention the Bible … we lose sales." "But the
> Pilgrims did read the Bible," [the author] answered. "Yes, you
> know that and we know that but we can't have anything in it that
> people object to."[52]

Finally, as regards history books, Vitz recounts the following:

> It is common in these books to treat Thanksgiving without
> explaining to whom the Pilgrims gave thanks. … The Pilgrims
> are described <u>entirely</u> without reference to religion. … So they
> had the first Thanksgiving. But no mention is made of the fact
> that it was God they were thanking. … One mother wrote me that
> her first grade son was told by the teacher that at Thanksgiving
> the Pilgrims gave thanks to the Indians! When she complained to
> the principal that Thanksgiving was a feast to thank God … the
> principal said that "they could only teach what was in the history
> books."[53]

The current situation in this country is a long way from the words of Patrick Henry:

> It cannot be emphasized too strongly or too often that this great
> nation was founded, not by religionists, but by Christians, not on
> religions, but on the Gospel of Jesus Christ! For this very reason
> peoples of other faiths have been offered asylum, prosperity and
> freedom of worship here.[54]

And those "other faiths" include secularists who do not believe in
extending to others the same liberties that have allowed them a place in
American society.

CHRISTIANITY AND THE PLAN OF GOVERNMENT

Nevertheless, in the founding documents of this nation – the Declaration
of Independence and the Constitution – the Christian assumptions and
perspectives that have made this country one of the most long-lasting
democracies in history remain. These are the gifts of Christianity to this
nation. They may be divided into five categories:

1. SEPARATION OF POWERS

All socialist plans of government are based on a vision of some kind of
utopianism. Even Christians face a temptation in this direction, as did the
Pilgrims, whose initial communal garden changed quickly to individual
household plots that were much more successful. They found that even
Christians will not work as hard for others as they will for themselves. In
other words, the Christian faith recognizes that we all are sinners; that, no
matter what our best intentions, we all find ourselves yielding to pride,
selfishness and greed. Recognizing, therefore, that we are all sinners –
perhaps the most basic concept of Christianity – the framers of the
Constitution set about to limit the effect of human sin upon its provisions
through a separation of powers, a system of checks and balances.

To begin with, the very enumeration of the powers of the national
government made the statement that its powers were *limited*. It simply
could not do whatever it wanted. The states also had powers, as did the
people.

The division of the national government into the three branches –
legislative, executive and judicial – is, perhaps, the most famous aspect of
the Constitution's separation of powers. Further, the legislative branch was
divided into two pieces: the House of Representatives, based on population,
and the Senate, giving equal representation to the states.

Then, the president may propose or veto legislation, but he cannot adopt it. He is the Commander in Chief, but the Congress must vote to declare war and fund it. The president selects federal judges, but the Senate must confirm them. Congress writes the laws, but the president must administer them. And over both branches, the legislative and executive, the federal courts are the watchdogs that make sure they do not exceed their constitutional powers.

Finally, the people elect, but they do not have the power to make or vote on laws. They must obey the laws made and enforced by those they elect. Yet, Congress can impeach representatives when those elected people engage in high crimes and misdemeanors.

The point of this brief civics lesson is that this system of checks and balances is derived directly from a Christian understanding of the nature of man. James Madison famously wrote, "If men were angels, there would be no need of government." Christianity understands the sinfulness of human beings, who, one and all, are in desperate need of fences to keep them from their worst selves. We do not have a Constitution that believes in unqualified human goodwill and righteousness. We do not have "hearts of gold" – even the best of us – so we need to check up on each other.

2. 'ENDOWED BY THEIR CREATOR'

This phrase from the Declaration of Independence tells the other side of the story. We have been created by a God who loves us and who, therefore, has "endowed" us with certain "unalienable rights" – specifically, "life, liberty, and the pursuit of happiness." There is an obvious connection between these three "rights." God has given us life, He wants us to be free and He wants us to be happy. These are the desires flowing from His love for us. And no one can legitimately take these rights away from us because God, Himself, has given them to us. They are "inalienable."

How do we know these things?

We know them because, as "Jesus Loves Me" tells us, "The Bible tells me so." It is as simple as that. Glenn Tinder, in *The Political Meaning of Christianity*, calls this the doctrine of "the exalted individual."[55] It is not something common sense has taught us, otherwise caste systems and slavery would not thrive in certain countries. The inherent worth of the individual reflected in American political theory is derived from America's Christian heritage and the beneficial influence of the Bible.

The terms "life, liberty, and happiness," "safety and happiness" and "future security" are all found in the Declaration of Independence. There is a God who made us and loves us. That is the source of these thoughts. He is our great shepherd. He wants us to be protected. And the basic purpose of government is to secure and protect these "inalienable rights" He has given us.

The Constitution reflects the same perspective when, in its preamble, it speaks of "justice, tranquility, the common defense, the general welfare and the blessings of liberty." All are provisions for human happiness. All are "blessings" intended for us by the God who made us and loves us. All are at the center of His scheme of things.

Sometimes we wonder what is at the root of the upbeat, optimistic spirit of this country. American optimism is founded, quite simply, on the love and care of God.

3. 'ALL MEN ARE CREATED EQUAL'

An explanation of this opening phrase of the Declaration of Independence flows from the foregoing section. It does not mean that all have equal intelligence, or beauty, or strength or family backgrounds, but it does mean that we have been "created equal" by our Creator. We are all equal before Him. He loves us equally.

So, the Constitution begins, "we the people of the United States." This is not a constitution of the elite made for all the serfs beneath them. As Abraham Lincoln said, this is a "government of the people, by the people, and for the people." This is our Constitution. In God's eyes, we all matter.

And so, too, the powers of government are derived powers. Derived from God, first,[56] and derived from the people, second. This is a government based on the consent of the governed. That is where equality comes in. As equals, we get together and form a government for ourselves. And from this equality also arises the right of rebellion against despotism that is found in the Declaration of Independence.

4. 'THE LAWS OF NATURE AND OF NATURE'S GOD'

These words of the Declaration of Independence form our historical basis for the concept of Natural Law. The laws spoken of here are not physical laws, such as the Law of Gravity, but moral laws. The point is that *we* do not make up these laws; these laws are given. They are God's laws. And they are found in the Bible *and* in nature, accessible to all in every culture and time.

C.S. Lewis explains this principle with great clarity in his book *Mere Christianity*. We don't decide that murder and stealing and betrayal are wrong, we discover these laws. Behind the natural order and human conscience, there is a sense in which these laws exist for us, not by us. They are a part of the "given" of creation.

5. TWO KINGDOMS

The New Testament says, "Render unto Caesar the things that are Caesar's and to God the things that are God's"[57] and "let every person be subject to the governing authorities."[58]

This is a doctrine that John Calvin famously emphasized – namely, a distinction between the kingdoms of the world and the Kingdom of heaven, between the realms of church and state. It is for this reason, among others, that the First Amendment was adopted and that Article VI of the Constitution concludes with the words,

> No religious test shall ever be required as a qualification to any
> Office or public Trust under the United States.

Christian Europe failed to adhere to this model, and religious strife resulted wherever the power of the state and the power of the church were joined in one institution. Our founders sought to avoid these mistakes when framing a new Constitution and, in adopting a different model, owe their basic ideas to Biblical concepts.

CONCLUSION

In 2002, 18 American tourists took a "Christian Heritage Tour" of China. One evening, a Chinese scholar from one of the nation's premier academic research institutes said in a lecture,

> One of the things we were asked to look into was what accounted
> for the success, in fact, the pre-eminence of the West all over
> the world. We studied everything we could from the historical,
> political and cultural perspective. At first we thought it was
> because you had more powerful guns than we had. Then we
> thought it was because you had the best political system. Next
> we focused on your economic system. But in the past 20 years,
> we have realized that the heart of your culture is your religion:
> Christianity. That is why the West has been so powerful. The
> Christian moral foundation of social and cultural life was

what made possible the emergence of capitalism and then the
successful transition to democratic politics. We don't have any
doubt about this.[59]

This is a remarkable analysis of the primary moral and cultural basis
of America in particular, and, by common heritage, of Western civilization
in general. It sounds almost as if it could have been written by Alexis de
Tocqueville.

It is difficult for us to comprehend, much less to value, the Christian
roots of this country because they seem so ordinary. But as soon as one
travels outside the United States long enough to gain an understanding of
the presuppositions of other governments, the blessings of our own become
clear. The psalmist says, "Blessed is the nation whose God is the Lord."[60]
And this nation is blessed because of its Godly heritage. Its principles flow
from Biblical principles.

"Every human being is a sinner and at the same time is loved by
God." This great idea served as the architectural framework of American
democracy, the framework on which our fundamental liberties have been
long supported.

CHAPTER SEVEN

CHRISTIANITY AND MORAL VALUES

In December 1989, the *Atlantic Monthly* published an article its editors won't soon forget because of the spate of cancelled subscriptions it caused. The article was by Glenn Tinder, then a professor of political science at the University of Massachusetts, and was titled, "Can We Be Good Without God?"[1] It dealt with one simple question: Can the moral values of the Christian faith long survive without belief in the faith that gave them birth? Tinder's answer: "To renew these indispensable values, I shall argue, we must rediscover their primal spiritual grounds."[2] Those spiritual grounds, he says, are found in the Christian faith. They are the "traditional" values of America.

Why do Americans believe, as our Founders said in the Declaration of Independence, that "all men are created equal?" Why do we believe that they are "endowed by their creator with certain unalienable rights" and "that among these are life, liberty, and the pursuit of happiness?" These great words contain moral values. Where do those values come from?

Descending to the nitty-gritty of everyday conduct, how do we know that pride, gossip, greed, lust, murder, lying, adultery, betrayal and revenge are wrong? How do we know that love, forgiveness, humility, honesty, faithfulness and patience are right? Where does this common understanding of negative and positive values come from?

There is only one historical answer to this question in the Western world. Our moral values come from God, imparted either through Natural Law, the moral understandings given by God that are instinctively possessed by all human beings, or imparted through Scripture, from which we gain detailed knowledge of God's holiness and His commands.

Here, then, is one of the most influential ideas of the Christian faith. The great idea, to borrow Glenn Tinder's words, is: *We cannot be good without God.*

GOD'S LOVE

In his remarkable article Tinder shows that the heart of Christian morality is Christianity's unique concept of love. It is not a concept found in ancient Greek or Roman philosophy, and so it is expressed in the Greek of the New Testament with a coined word, found exclusively in the New Testament and then in the writings of the early Christian Fathers. It is the word *agape*. *Agape* is self-sacrificing, self-originating love that is not prompted by the value of its object but, instead, confers value upon its object.

First and foremost, *agape* is a characteristic of Divine love, according to the New Testament. It is at the core of Christian morality and also at the heart of how we should treat each other as human beings. It means there is a certain "glory" in every individual, the glory of being the object of God's love. As Tinder puts it, "The Christian universe is peopled exclusively with royalty."[3] In ancient times, Greeks and Hebrews saw outsiders as beneath them – but that has never been true of Christians. In Christianity, all are worthy of being loved because all are objects of God's love. The implications of this perspective are enormous.

Recently, the *Wall Street Journal* ran an article on how small businesses are faring in Russia.[4] As a case in point, the article followed the misfortunes of Mariana Ivashina, the founder and owner of a small, local baby food business. When she complained to the Kremlin about bureaucratic meddling in her business on the part of the local government, her bank account was frozen and her business folded. When, shortly afterward, she was made head of the local branch of the national small business association, she began to get 400 calls a day from local businesses complaining about endless inspections by firemen, sanitation inspectors and policemen, who would invent violations as a means of soliciting bribes. She wrote an article in a local paper, which she founded, laying out a "price list" of bribes: $100 for the inspection of a new business, $5,000 up front for a contract to rent space in a municipal building. When warned in an anonymous phone call not to publish the article, she refused to back down. On the morning it was published, she was attacked by two youths with brass knuckles. In a poll, 70 percent of Russian small business owners said their chances of protecting their lawful interests in court were slim to none.

In a society like Russia today, where any memory of Christian moral principles is lost in the deep, dark past prior to the advent of communism, morality is exchanged for power and wealth and a whole society becomes impossibly corrupt. Theft, bribery, lies, physical intimidation and every kind of corruption become commonplace, while the idea that there is a certain "glory" in even the most common of individuals becomes laughable. No one believes it or treats others as if they believe it. As Dostoyevsky said famously in *The Brothers Karamazov*, when there is no God, "everything is permitted."

There are certain things most Westerners have historically agreed are wrong, even though other cultures permit them. A list of such things would include polygamy, bribery, slavery, incest, plagiarism, homosexuality and pedophilia. Why? Not because everyone has "figured it out" in a triumph of individual reason, but because of the residue of a Christian moral legacy. When we think "moral values" in the West, whether we know it or not, to a large extent we are thinking "Christian moral values."

The landscape of the West, in general, and of the United States, in particular, is dotted with Christianity-based orphanages, hospitals, schools, homeless shelters, relief organizations and public service agencies such as the YMCA, the YWCA and the Red Cross. This is not happenstance. This is a product of the great idea that we cannot be good without God, as well as the great idea that every human being – though a sinner – is loved by God. As just one example, Hindu India, where sickness, health and human individuality are regarded as illusions, has not produced a similar tradition of humanitarianism.

BIBLICAL SOURCES

The Biblical connection between God and moral values is so obvious that it may seem superfluous even to mention it, but it is important to lay the groundwork for some examples. Here is one from I Peter:

Therefore, gird up your minds, be sober, set your hope fully upon
the grace that is coming to you at the revelation of Jesus Christ.
As obedient children, do not be conformed to the passions of
your former ignorance, but as He who called you is holy, be holy
yourselves in all your conduct.[5]

Essentially, Peter is saying, based on God's great love and the salvation
He has given us in Jesus Christ, I have something important I want to say
to you ("therefore").

Let's take a deep breath and think clearly about the implications of this
("Gird up your minds, be sober").

Focus on what wonderful things are going to happen when we meet
Jesus in the life to come ("Set your hope fully upon the grace that is coming
to you at the revelation of Jesus Christ").

As God's children through Jesus, do not live like you once did in the
passions and ignorance of your lives before you knew any better ("As
obedient children, do not be conformed to the passions of your former
ignorance").

But as God is now your Father, live a new life in which your aim is to
become more and more like Him ("But as He who called you is holy, be
holy yourselves in all your conduct").

The connection here between the morality of Christians and their belief
in God could not be clearer. The idea is, "We love because He first loved
us."[6] The "belief" part is that God loves them and has made them His
children. The "morality" part is that He is now their Father, and they want
to be like Him. Moreover, they'll be going home to Him soon – their real
home is heaven.

The idea of living here and now as grateful children of the heavenly
Father, and as citizens of heaven – living into one's destiny – is the theme
not only of I Peter 1, but also of Ephesians 4-6, Philippians 3, Galatians
5, Colossians 3 and other New Testament passages. Obeying our Father is
the normal day-to-day response of Christians and is motivated in the New
Testament both by God's love in Christ and by the prospect of soon being
in heaven.

As Paul says in Romans 12:1, 2:

I appeal to you therefore, brethren, by the mercies of God, to
present your bodies as a living sacrifice, holy and acceptable to
God.

God's forgiving love is the motive, sacrificial living is the result. In so saying, Paul is echoing the words of Jesus in Mark 8:34, 35:

> If any man would come after me, let him deny himself and take up his cross daily and follow me. For whoever would save his life will lose it and whoever loses his life for my sake and the Gospel's will save it.

EARLY AMERICA

Virtually all of the Founding Fathers made this connection between moral values and the Christian faith. George Washington often spoke of "religion" and "morality" in the same breath. In his famous 1796 "Farewell Address" at the end of his presidency, he said,

> Religion and morality are indispensable supports. ... Reason and experience both forbid us to expect that national morality can prevail in exclusion of religious principle. ... Cultivate peace and harmony with all. Religion and morality enjoin this conduct.[7]

In his circular address to the states in 1783, Washington spoke of "the pure and benign light of Revelation" which, he said, had had "a meliorating influence on mankind and increased the blessings of society."[8] He concluded with the following prayer:

> I now make it my earnest prayer, that God would have you, and the State over which you preside, in His holy protection, that He would incline the hearts of the Citizens to cultivate a spirit of subordination and obedience to government, to entertain a brotherly affection and love for one another ... and finally, that He would most graciously dispose us all to do justice, love mercy, and to demean ourselves with that charity, humility and pacific temper of mind, which were the characteristics of the Divine Author of our blessed Religion.[9]

John Adams made the same connection between the Christian religion and morality. In an 1813 letter to Thomas Jefferson, he speaks of "the general principles of Christianity" as being the principles on which America was founded.[10]

Jefferson and Benjamin Franklin are often singled out as the deists among the Founding Fathers, but they were not deists by any modern definition. Jefferson, for example, writes,

Can the liberties of a nation be thought secure when we have
removed their only firm basis, a conviction in the minds of the
people that these liberties are the gift of God? That they are not to
be violated but with His wrath? Indeed I tremble for my country
when I reflect that God is just.[11]

Franklin wrote:

Doing good to men is the only service of God in our power and to
imitate His beneficence is to glorify Him.[12]

Notice in both quotations the cause-and-effect connection between
religion and morality.

MORAL VALUES WITHOUT RELIGION

Fast forward to the present. Hadley Arkes, a professor of American
Institutions at Amherst College, in his book, *Natural Rights and the Right
to Choose*, speaks of one of the most infamous decisions in the history
of the U.S. Supreme Court, the Dred Scott case of 1856 that upheld the
institution of slavery. Arkes quotes the dissenting opinion of Justice John
McLean, who speaks of the black man in these words, "He bears the
impress of his Maker and is amenable to the laws of God and Man; and he
is destined to an endless existence."[13] Arkes comments, "He has, in other
words, a soul, which is imperishable."

He then refers to some academic colleagues who sometimes speak about
the "sanctity" of a homeless man in the gutter. And he asks, "Sanctity? Do
they mean of the sacred? Does that not rather point to, well, You-know-
who?"

My colleagues in the academy speak firmly of "rights," or of the
"injuries" done to "persons," and they seem serenely unaware that
their language here is grounded in understandings that they have
professed, at least, to have rejected long ago.[14]

Then he exposes the inconsistency of their atheism:

They cannot possibly give the same account of the wrong of
slavery ... that McLean was in a position to give. ... The modern
liberal will proclaim his social sympathy and strike a militant
posture in defense of rights, but he can no longer explain why that
biped who conjugates verbs should be the bearer of rights.[15]

The point is, the connection between morality and religion is waning in many modern academic circles. "Many people," Arkes says, "have gradually talked themselves out of the ground of their rights without quite being aware of it. For like those professors in the academy, they can no longer offer a moral defense of those rights; and worse than that, they have talked themselves into premises quite at odds with the premises of the American Founders. To put it another way, they have talked themselves out of the premises on which their own freedom rests."[16]

In some parts of today's world, in other words, the great idea of the Founders that we cannot be good without God, the idea that belief in a God who is holy is the indispensable basis of moral standards, has been replaced by a new "great idea" – the notion that all moral standards are relative. Though the man on the street may not be familiar with that notion, he has at least heard from others that he must never be "judgmental" of the values of others because one value is as good as another. Still, most "men on the street" are smarter than that. They know there must be some absolutes in life.

Nevertheless, the whole "moral values" scene is a chaotic mess. People make up their own values, and no one is allowed to "judge" those values.

'THE SWEET MYSTERY OF LIFE'

In its own way, the U.S. Supreme Court has put its stamp of approval on the moral confusion that has trickled down into society from the intellectual elite – the confusion produced by the idea that all values are personal, tentative and provisional, made up out of whole cloth if need be, completely disconnected from any particular idea of religion and God, but based on individual "reason" alone.

In this regard, the members of the Supreme Court (with some notable exceptions) are children of their age. Their imprimatur on the idea of a valueless society was given in the *Planned Parenthood v. Casey* decision, written by Justice Anthony Kennedy in 1992. The decision began,

> Some of us as individuals find abortion offensive to our most
> basic principles of morality, but that cannot control our decision.
> Our obligation is to define the liberty of all, not to mandate our
> own moral code.[17]

The majority opinion went on to reason that our law affords constitutional protection to "the most intimate and personal choices a person may make in a lifetime, choices central to personal dignity and autonomy, [which] are central to the liberty protected by the Fourteenth Amendment."[18]

Then comes the famous "Sweet Mystery of Life" passage of the opinion: "At the heart of liberty is the right to define one's own concept of existence, of meaning, of the universe, and of the mystery of human life."

Justice Antonin Scalia, in a dissenting opinion, commented on those words:

> I have never heard of a law that attempted to restrict one's "right to define" certain concepts; and if the passage calls into question the government's power to regulate actions based on one's self-defined "concept of existence, etc.," it is the passage that ate the rule of law.[19]

Judge Robert H. Bork, one of President Ronald Reagan's unsuccessful nominees to the Supreme Court, commented, "Reading these words, it is hard to know what there is left for legislatures to do, since each individual is now a sovereign nation."[20]

Perhaps the most appropriate comment of all is found in the last verse of Judges: "In those days there was no king in Israel; every man did what was right in his own eyes."[21]

We live in a time of moral relativism to which the highest levels of the judiciary have acceded. It is a dangerous time and a situation far removed from the intent of the Founding Fathers. As Bork has put it,

> The anarchical spirit of extreme personal and group autonomy … is the driving force behind much of our cultural degradation. Call it what you will – moral chaos, relativism, postmodernism – extreme issues of autonomy already suffuse our culture quite aside from any assistance from the courts.[22]

THE TWO TABLES OF THE LAW

In order to understand the contribution made to the public good by linking morality to God, it is worth offering two examples of what happens when that link is broken. To do that let's refer, for a moment, to the most familiar Biblical moral ground, the first and second "great" commandments and the "10 Commandments" that follow their outline.

The Law of God may be said to be divided into two main parts – our obligations toward God and our obligations toward one another. In one of the most famous passages of the New Testament, Jesus is asked by a scholar, "Teacher, which is the great commandment of the law?" Jesus replies, "You shall love the Lord your God with all your heart, and with all your soul, and with all your mind. This is the great and first commandment." Then Jesus immediately adds: "And a second is like it, you shall love your neighbor as yourself." He concludes, "On these two commandments depend all the law and the prophets."[23]

Similarly, the Ten Commandments follow this two-part outline: the first five having to do with our relationship with God and the second five with our relationship with our neighbor.

THE FIRST TABLE OF THE LAW

The first five commandments[24] contain about 200 words – the second five,[25] about 50. Unquestionably, our relationship with God is of primary importance – not only because it is mentioned first but because it is explained at much greater length.

The first five commands (using the Protestant, rather than the Roman Catholic numbering) are these, in brief:

1. You shall have no other gods.
2. You shall not make and worship any images or idols.
3. You shall not take God's name in vain.
4. Remember the Sabbath day, to keep it holy.
5. Honor your father and your mother.

Of the first five commands, there is only one about which there may be any question concerning its inclusion in the first "table" or tablet, the table relating to our duty toward God. That is the fifth, which concerns honoring parents. In fact, it fits well in the first table because honoring one's parents has everything to do with honoring God.

We tend to think about our heavenly parent in terms of our experience with our earthly parents. And to honor our father and mother – however we may feel toward them at the moment – teaches us to honor our Father in heaven. Family illustrations of love, faithfulness and loyalty fill the Bible as God's way of teaching us about our relationship with Him.

ISSUES REGARDING THE FAMILY

In the fifth commandment, the family command, we find Christian moral values to be very much at odds with the clamor for different values from various segments of society.

A recent article in the *Lake Champlain Weekly*, "Church For Sale," told of the catastrophic decline in Catholic church attendance in Quebec from 1960s averages of 80-to-90 percent to a current average of less than eight. The article then says, "The decline ... is also reflected in the province's record-low birth rate, increased abortion rate, single parent homes, divorce rates and reluctance to marry."[26]

These problems are not unknown in the United States. The family is declining and, without immigration, the country would have a negative growth rate. The American divorce rate hovers around 50 percent. Only 15 percent of the population agrees that "when there are children in the family, parents should stay together even if they don't get along." As many as two-thirds of divorces are for "soft" reasons, such as vague feelings of unhappiness, rather than "hard" reasons, such as high conflict, adultery or abuse. The percentage of households with children has dropped from 62 percent in 1960 to 43 percent in 1985, and the projection for 2010 is 25 percent. In 1998, 19 percent of women aged 40-44 were childless, compared to 10 percent in 1980. About one-third of children are being raised in fatherless homes, a predictor of school problems, drug use and criminal behavior. In some segments of the population, 70 percent of the children are fatherless.

But we don't really need statistics. All we need to do is look around us to see couples living together before marriage, couples waiting longer to commit to marriage and couples waiting still longer to have children. In large numbers, people seem to be opting out of marriage altogether and, if they do marry, opting out of having children altogether. Families are smaller. One-child families are on the rise.[27]

What all of this means is that one of the deepest sources of human happiness, marrying and having children – and one day having lots of wonderful grandchildren – just is not happening for many people today.

Adding to these problems is a strong contemporary push to redefine American marriage. Several state legislatures have added defense of marriage amendments to their state constitutions, which would limit marriage to its traditional scope: one man and one woman taking vows to each other to live together as husband and wife.

The issue raises all kinds of questions with no simple solutions. Don't we believe in civil rights? And don't we specifically believe in civil rights for gays and lesbians? Isn't marriage a civil right for all? We believe in civil rights for adulterers, don't we? Why not civil rights for gays and lesbians?

And we don't believe that children are mandatory in marriage, do we? The Bible simply says that a man shall leave his father and mother, cleave to his wife and the two shall become one flesh. And we have no problem with two people who are past childbearing age getting married. So, why do we have a problem with same-sex marriage? Marriage doesn't have to mean there are children. Why can't we just lighten up and cease our opposition to same-sex marriage as a civil right?

The answer goes well beyond the Biblical condemnations of homosexuality in Romans 1 and I Corinthians 6 to the deeper issue of what marriage is and the connection between marriage and family.

Here are some thoughts to ponder before we support civil legislation to redefine marriage to include gays and lesbians or fail to support a National Marriage Amendment.

First of all, traditional marriage is a universal human institution, and we should at least pause before we redefine it. Maggie Gallagher, one of the leaders of the modern marriage movement, has said,

> In all the wildly rich and various cultures flung throughout the ecosphere, in society after society, whether tribal or complex, and however bizarre, human beings have created systems of publicly approved sexual union between men and women that entail well-defined responsibilities of mothers and fathers. Not all these marriage systems look like our own ... yet everywhere, in isolated mountain valleys, parched deserts, jungle thickets and broad plains, people have come up with some version of this thing called marriage.[28]

This should at least be a flashing yellow light for us before we start tinkering. Let's be careful before we change what marriage always has been.

Secondly, if unions of gays and lesbians are to be included in our new definition of marriage, what prejudice allows us to leave out bisexuals? Others speak of GLBT (gay, lesbian, bisexual and transgendered) issues. Why stop by admitting only gays and lesbians to the marriage club? And if marital threesomes are to be allowed, as a sensitivity to bisexuality might imply, what about polygamy? We may think this is a non-issue in the Western world, but it was only 150 years ago, when mainstream Mormons were still polygamous, that it was a very significant issue here in the United States. In all seriousness, do we really think a pitched battle for polygamy would be lost today? Federal troops were dispatched to the Utah territory and the Mormons had to abandon polygamy as a condition of statehood. But that might not happen today.

Thirdly, why not just let people live together and take vows to each other privately as they wish? Why does the state need to be involved in this at all? The issue is not about taxes. As we all know, married couples in this country sometimes pay a tax *penalty* for being married. The issue is not about benefits. Out of 1.3 million employees of General Motors, only 166 have claimed benefits for a same-sex partner. That's 0.002 percent. And if gays and lesbians are two percent of the population, that means that only one in a hundred gays and lesbians used this option. And this was possible *without* a change in the civil definition of marriage![29]

Let's back up one step. What is the most basic universal definition of marriage?

Try this on for size: Marriage is the primary cultural institution through which one generation bears and nurtures the next. Does this mean everyone who gets married has to have a baby? Not at all, but it does mean that this is what marriage as a human institution is primarily about.

Here is how Maggie Gallagher puts it:

> Why is marriage a universal human institution? Because sex
> between men and women makes babies, that's why. Even today,
> in our technologically advanced contraceptive culture, half of all
> pregnancies are unintended: sex between men and women *still*
> makes babies.[30]

What really is at stake here is not only marriage, but also the family.

So, what happens in societies where marriage is redefined to include the unions of gays and lesbians?

The answer in Scandinavian countries, where the legalization of homosexual unions began 15 years ago, is that marriage declines and a majority of children are born out of wedlock.[31] In the United States, we think the fact that one-third of children are born out of wedlock is a serious problem.

What is the role of gay marriage in all of this? Stanley Kurtz, a research fellow at the Hoover Institution, says, "Scandinavian gay marriage has driven home the message that marriage itself is outdated and virtually any family form, including out-of-wedlock parenthood, is acceptable."[32] Gene Edward Veith, a family researcher, says, "Homosexual marriage has contributed to the dissolution of marriage as a significant institution in

Scandinavian cultures primarily by contributing to the notion that marriage need have nothing to do with children."[33]

Finally, a 2000 study by Yale's William Eskridge showed that, after achieving legal approval, gay unions declined sharply in Scandinavia to annual figures of 265 in Denmark, 200 in Sweden and 190 in Norway – indicating that the real issue in the present debate is official cultural approval of homosexuality, not the right to marry.[34]

On June 10, 2003, the highest court in Ontario, Canada, endorsed same-sex marriage. In its struggle to redefine marriage, it said,

> Marriage is, without dispute, one of the most significant forms
> of personal relationship. ... Through the institution of marriage,
> individuals can publicly express their love and commitment to
> each other. Through this institution, society publicly recognizes
> expressions of love and commitment between individuals,
> granting them respect and legitimacy as a couple.

But marriage as a cultural institution has always been more than this. It has always been, in fact, the primary cultural institution by which one generation bears and nurtures the next.

It has never been only a recognition of expressions of love between individuals. Marriage has to do with families. Families involve children, and the way we define families has everything to do with the future of our culture.

Cultural approval of same-sex marriage is one step beyond civil rights for homosexuals. If the cost of that cultural approval is a radical redefinition of marriage that seriously undermines the family, the cost will be far too high.

Let's stick with the marriage definition of Jesus and Genesis. As Jesus explained in Mark 10:6, 7,

> From the beginning of creation "God made them male and
> female." For this reason a man shall leave his father and mother
> and be joined to his wife and the two shall become one flesh. So
> they are no longer two but one flesh.

And, of course, children normally will result – as they did for Adam and Eve. That is what marriage is. Only if we keep marriage as it is will it continue to reflect the security, love and loyalty found in our relationship with God. Only if we keep marriage as it is will it continue to bless us with the happiness of lifelong family relationships.

THE SECOND TABLE OF THE LAW

The second five commandments have to do with our relationship with our neighbor:

1. You shall not kill.
2. You shall not commit adultery.
3. You shall not steal.
4. You shall not bear false witness.
5. You shall not covet.

One of these commands, the sixth, is central to today's abortion controversy. The question which, more than any other, is holding up nominations to the U.S. Supreme Court and the federal judiciary is, to be very plain, "When is it okay to kill a baby?" Opinions differ radically. The starkest division is between those who say "sometimes" and those who say "never."

There is a wide variation among those who say "sometimes." At one end of the spectrum is Professor Peter Singer of Princeton University, who has famously held that parents should be able to kill their own babies within the first three months of life.

Others have held that, in the relatively rare case of an abortion in which the baby is mistakenly born alive, a baby may be killed in the first day or so of life. As Hadley Arkes has described it, "One federal judge had famously opined that even a child who had survived an abortion was not protected by the law: It was a fetus marked for 'termination.'"[35]

The method used in these cases is "exposure." Specifically, the child is left on a table in a back room to die. This "procedure" first came to public notice through the testimony of Jill Stanek, then a nurse at Christ Hospital in Oak Lawn, Illinois. At first thought to be a one-of-a-kind case, Stanek was later interviewed on a national radio talk show and calls came in from nurses all over the country "who testified that these kinds of abortions had been practiced at their hospitals for years."[36]

What a mockery this practice makes of the command to "love" your neighbor as yourself! Those babies were not loved.

In July 2000, a bill was introduced in the U.S. Senate to make this procedure illegal, and it was immediately opposed by the National Abortion Rights Action League. Nevertheless, the bill passed both houses of Congress and, in a private White House ceremony in August 2002,

President George W. Bush signed the "Born Alive Infant's Protection Act,"[37] the first law against abortion to withstand constitutional challenge – or, at least, no challenge has yet been made.

Others have held that abortions should be allowed only up to, but not including, birth – that even if the baby is partially born, with its feet dangling into the world, the baby has not yet seen, so it is still okay to kill him or her. The colloquial name for this procedure is partial birth abortion, while the technical name is dilation and extraction.

In 1995, both houses of Congress passed a bill banning this procedure, which was vetoed two weeks later by President William Clinton. By 1998, nearly 20 states had passed bills outlawing the procedure. In 2000, the issue was brought before the U.S. Supreme Court, which struck down all the state bans in *Stenberg v. Carhart*.[38] However, the federal government enacted the Partial-Birth Abortion Ban Act in 2003. After various challenges and adjustments, it was eventually upheld by the Supreme Court in *Gonzales v. Carhart* (2007).

Whether inside or outside the womb, the issue in all of these cases is whether a baby is a human being. Presently, we find ourselves in the untenable position of having to rely completely on the Supreme Court for an answer to this question: Who is a human being with protected rights? As Hadley Arkes has pointed out, it reminds one of a tragically illuminating episode from *Huckleberry Finn* in which Huck has made up a story as to why his boat was delayed.

He says to Aunt Sally, "We blowed out a cylinder-head."

Aunt Sally says, "Good gracious! Anybody hurt?"

Huck says, "No'm. Killed a nigger."

Aunt Sally concludes: "Well, it's lucky; because sometimes people do get hurt."[39]

Neither Huck nor Aunt Sally, you see, considered a black man to be a human being.

In the same way, many in the courts today do not consider infants to be human beings who feel, cry or experience pain – much less possess a destiny. Thanks to the institution of abortion, they are just fetuses, whether inside or outside the womb.[40]

Nevertheless, almost 70 percent of the public supports a ban on partial-birth abortion.[41] Ordinary people know it is against God's law to kill babies. "Thou shalt not kill." We all learned it when we first memorized the Ten Commandments in Sunday school. And, when a child asks any pregnant mother, "What's in there?" she will reply, "a baby" – not "a fetus." She feels it move. More often than not, she knows what sex it is. She has seen it already in one or more ultrasounds. And in many cases, weeks before birth, it already has a name. The baby is loved. She is a human being with a God-given destiny – an object of God's fatherly, unwavering love.

We cannot be good without God. It is somehow only when God has been edged out of the equation that we are willing to fall for the lie that only courts know whether, or in what circumstances, a baby is a human being.

One of the research conclusions – as if it were necessary – that has been firmly reached in the whole abortion controversy is that infants, born and unborn, feel pain. At the most elemental level, "love thy neighbor as thyself" therefore means that, if I love myself enough not to want a doctor to take "a pair of blunt curved Metzenbaum scissors" and "force the scissors into the base of the skull" of my own head, "spread the scissors to enlarge the opening" and "introduce a suction catheter into this hole and evacuate the skull contents,"[42] then I sure am not going to let him do that to a baby.

Scripture reveals a special place in God's heart for the "widows and the fatherless,"[43] a special love and concern for the weak and defenseless in this world, but somehow many of us only adopt this perspective when God enters the picture and His will guides our moral compass. There also is, of course, the special prohibition in Scripture – in the Ten Commandments – against murder.

In the Roman world of New Testament times, both abortion and infanticide were widely practiced. The relevant contemporary literature describes an amazingly varied number of abortion techniques.[44] As was the case with the Emperor Domitian, the abortion decision today is not necessarily made by the woman who possesses the vaunted freedom of choice but, instead, by the man or men in her life. Domitian, having impregnated his niece, Julia, ordered her to have an abortion, from which she died.[45]

From earliest times, Christians in the Roman Empire set themselves apart by absolutely prohibiting abortion and infanticide. In the second century, for example, Athenagoras wrote:

> We say that women who use drugs to bring on an abortion
> commit murder, and will have to give an account to God for the

abortion ... [for we] regard the very foetus in the womb as a created being, and therefore an object of God's care ... and [we do not] expose an infant, because those who expose them are chargeable with child murder.[46]

CONCLUSION

Some people have likened the Christian faith to perfume in a vial. On the one hand, the perfume represents the faith itself – the knowledge of God's love and Christ's sacrifice and His invitation, "Come to me all who labor and are heavy laden and I will give you rest. Take my yoke upon you and learn of me for I am gentle and lowly in heart and you will find rest for your souls."[47] On the other hand, the odor represents the life and love that emanates from that faith. And the question is, for how long can a culture live on the perfume of an empty vial?

Where our culture is moving in the future in the whole arena of moral values may be an unanswerable question, but where we have come from is no mystery. The unique concept of love found in the Biblical word *agape* is the foundation of the moral history of the Western world. It is the nature of God Himself that is at the basis of our moral values.

The Founders believed in the great idea of the Christian faith, that "we cannot be good without God." As George Washington reminded in his Farewell Address (1796):

> ... let us with caution indulge the supposition that morality can be maintained without religion, ... reason and experience both forbid us to expect that national morality can prevail in exclusion of religious principle.

To divorce morality from religion, as those who exalt individual autonomy above all else do, is to risk cultural disintegration. We may live off the memory of inherited Biblical values for a time but, like perfume from an empty vial, the fragrance will eventually fade entirely. If it does, if the vial is not replenished by nurturing the great ideas on which the West was built, the self-restraint essential to self-government may vanish with it – or so the Founders believed.

CHAPTER EIGHT

NEGATIVES

In his book, *The End of Faith: Religion, Terror and the Future of Reason,* Sam Harris lobbies hard for the notion that all terrorism is religiously based, that religion presents the greatest danger to world peace and that, if we do not grow up soon and replace the errors of religion with clear-headed reason, the future for this world looks pretty bleak.

He opens with a chillingly matter-of-fact description of the last day in the life of a suicide bomber.[1] He then tells where his book is going:

> A glance at history … reveals that ideas which divide one group
> of human beings from another, only to unite them in slaughter,
> generally have their roots in religion. … Intolerance is intrinsic
> to every creed. … Our religious differences are antithetical to our
> survival.[2]

His approach is so wrong and yet so widely shared that it seems best to approach it at the outset with some obvious truths:

- Not all religions are the same.

- Not all religions, therefore, hold the same danger of conflict.

- Not all fundamentalisms within religions are equally dangerous. (Mennonite "fundamentalism" would surely be pacifist.)

- Not all orthodox movements are fundamentalist. (The term "fundamentalist" in American Christianity has a very specific

historical meaning that would lead many people who claim to
be "orthodox" or "evangelical" to reject it as a description of
themselves.)

- Not all those who claim to be Christians are (as defined in the
  Biblical sense).

- Not all Christians act like Christians should, and even the most
  faithful Christians have personal failures. Christianity is a religion
  of forgiveness.

- Christians do not claim to follow all the examples and commands
  found in the Old Testament for a score of different reasons
  (for example, Old Testament religion was a theocracy,
  New Testament religion was not).

The old canard that religion has been the cause of all historical conflicts
is simplistic and meaningless. In the 20th century, Adolf Hitler, Josef
Stalin, Mao Tse Tung and Pol Pot were all atheists of one sort or another
and, together, were responsible for somewhere in the range of 100 million
violent deaths. Are we to say that the religion of atheism is responsible?
Perhaps, but it is not very helpful to say it. It is just too simplistic. And
atheism would probably not be classified as a religion by people like Sam
Harris anyway – though, to the extent that it is a worldview, it certainly is.

Nevertheless, the Christian faith has always been attacked for certain
"negative" historical events. Any book that honestly expounds the great
benefits of the ideas of the Christian faith should also pause for a moment
to look at some of these.

They are primarily four in number: the Crusades, anti-Semitism, witch-
hunts and the Spanish Inquisition. These are the blots on Christianity one
hears about most often. What can be said about them? The answers given
here are not intended to be exhaustive or complete, but to suggest the broad
general direction in which the answers may be found.

THE CRUSADES

On November 27, 1095, Pope Urban II addressed a great crowd in
the city of Clermont, France. There was widespread anger over the recent
persecution of pilgrims to the Holy Land and, for the pontiff, enough was
enough. So, he told the crowd:

If you must have blood, bathe in the blood of infidels. ... Become

> soldiers of the Living God. ... It is Christ Himself who comes
> from the tomb and presents you with this cause. ... Wear it upon
> your shoulders and your breasts.[3]

The crowd began to cut cloth into the famous crusaders' crosses that were then sewn on their garments and became the emblem of the four Crusades to the Holy Land. On that day, a great volunteer movement began to take back the Holy Land for Christ. Why?

In Christianity, history matters. Christ, the Son of God, entered the world at a specific place and time, lived in a specific place and time for 30-some years, was crucified and raised from death – again, at a very specific place and time. So, the historic places where He lived, died and rose became very important places to Christians. These physical places supported the realities of the faith. Thus, when Christianity became the majority religion of the Roman Empire, under Emperor Constantine (280-337), actions were taken to preserve and commemorate this history.

Jerusalem was a part of his empire, so Constantine erected a huge basilica over the site of the tomb where Christ was believed to have been placed before His resurrection, the Church of the Holy Sepulchre.

Understandably, it became the holiest of all Christian shrines in ensuing centuries. As Sir Steven Runciman said in his three-volume history of the Crusades,

> An unending stream of travelers poured eastward, sometimes
> traveling in parties numbering thousands, men and women of
> every age and every class ready ... to spend a year or more on the
> [journey].[4]

In the Holy Land, people climbed the hill where Christ had died; they visited His birthplace in Bethlehem; they viewed the scenery He looked at when He walked this earth; they "touched Him" in walking where He walked.

Toward the end of the first millennium, however, the Middle East was overrun by the conquering hordes of Islam and, in 1009, Muslims destroyed the Church of the Holy Sepulchre. Later in that century, the Turks, recent converts to Islam, began to waylay Christian pilgrims. Many were extorted for "tolls" along the way, seized and sold into slavery or tortured and killed.

As the Muslim Turks spread across the Anatolian peninsula, they came within a hundred miles of Constantinople, and the emperor of Byzantium wrote to his fellow Christians in the West for help. He told of the gruesome torture of Christians, of the desecration of churches and of impending conquest. He predicted that if Constantinople were finally overrun by the Muslim conquerors, not only would Christians be murdered, tortured and raped, but "the most holy relics of the Savior" would be lost. "Therefore," the emperor said, "in the name of God ... we implore you to bring to this city all the faithful soldiers of Christ." It was this letter that was the basis of Pope Urban's famous speech.[5]

The Crusades, therefore, did not begin without cause. They were, in fact, a defensive action against Muslim conquest and a reaction to the subsequent closure of access to Christian touchstones that the militant nature of Islam had brought upon itself.[6]

Four great volunteer attempts to solve this two-pronged problem followed: the first Crusade of 1095-1099, the second of 1146-1149, the third of 1188-1192, and the Shepherds Crusade of 1320. The Crusades were, variously, a defensive, reforming and missionary endeavor. Thousands of preachers spread the pope's message of Christian devotion and solidarity. The all-volunteer armies were entirely self-funded. Preachers and Crusaders alike were motivated by the glory of Christ. Rightly or wrongly, they were men deeply committed to Catholic orthodoxy. And their preaching was as much against the indolence of the clergy at home as it was against the conquering Muslims abroad.[7] It was not a fight they had started, but it was one they entered with holy enthusiasm. The impression often found today, however, is that the Crusades were just exhibits of raw Christian aggression. And that simply is not the whole story.

ANTI-SEMITISM

The fallout from the zeal of the Crusades included a reformation of the Church and a wave of Jewish massacres.[8] The connection, in the words of one historian, was this:

> When a truly significant threat arose, as Christian Europe initiated war with Islam, toleration even of non-threatening religious non-conformity was withdrawn. As a French abbot put it, "What is the good of going to the end of the world at great loss of men and money, to fight Saracens [Muslims], when we permit among us other infidels who are a thousand times more guilty toward Christ than are the Mohammedans."[9]

This logic, of course, is faulty for several reasons, but reason is often in short supply in times of great emotion.

The fact is, the rise of anti-Semitism came at the end of "tranquil centuries" in the relationship between Christians and Jews in Europe. In the first three or four centuries of the Christian Church, one of the primary networks for the spread of the Gospel was Hellenistic Judaism – that is, Jews who had settled around the Mediterranean Sea far from the center of Judaism in Jerusalem; Jews who may never have been to Jerusalem and did not speak Hebrew; Jews who were fully a part of the Greek classical culture of the Roman Empire. The close connection between Judaism and Christianity found in the New Testament – in the sense that the Apostle Paul always went first to the synagogue to preach when he entered a new city and often wrote his letters with new Jewish converts in view – continued into the fourth century. Throughout those first 400 years, a large proportion of the Christian Church was made up of first-generation Jewish converts.[10]

So, there was virtually no anti-Semitism in the Church for its first 400 years. In the next 600 years of the first millennium, this "tranquil" relationship continued. Jews and Christians lived side by side, with Jews worshiping in synagogues and celebrating Old Testament holidays.[11]

But the Crusades changed all that. In 1096, bands of soldiers who had gathered for the First Crusade attacked Jews in numerous towns along the Rhine River. In one, the local Catholic bishop saved most of them by bringing them into his own palace. When Worms' bishop attempted to do the same thing, the soldiers broke down his gate and murdered 500 Jews. Time and again the bishops attempted to protect the Jews, often in vain.[12]

The bishops' resistance indicates that the hordes of Crusaders were out of control and unable to be appeased even by the Church for which they were embarking on a journey of war. There were, of course, no mass media and no printing presses in those days. News and its interpretation traveled slowly, by word of mouth. Any movement at any moment could veer out of control.

During the First Crusade, perhaps 5,500 Jews were killed in Europe before the soldiers left for the trek to the Holy Land. More were killed in a synagogue in Jerusalem during the massacre of Muslims there. In the remaining Crusades, the number of Jews killed was far less.

Later, when Spain was retaken from the Muslims, more Jews were killed, and still later, when the Black Death stalked Europe, even more

Jews were killed in a kind of thoughtless revenge for the lives of those taken by disease. This was not Church-sanctioned slaughter but, rather, the ignorant response of peasants seeking to scapegoat "strangers" for the plague that had befallen them.

In more recent times, it is widely known that the complicity of the German Catholic church in World War II's Holocaust was no greater than the complicity of the German Lutheran church. This was a time of cultural madness in Germany in which virtually the entire nation was swept up in a Holocaust that had far more to do with the influence of Darwin (and consequent evolutionary eugenics) and Nietzsche (in whose writings godless power replaced Christian morality) than it did with the Christian faith. Christians often looked the other way in fear, but their beliefs were not the source of the ideologies that created the problem.

Many Christians, of course, did not look the other way. Dietrich Bonhoeffer, a well-known Christian theologian, was one of many people who joined in the German underground resistance against Hitler and was executed just days before the end of World War II. Corrie ten Boom, a Dutch lady, joined with her parents and sister in hiding a Jewish family in their home, as did thousands of others. She wrote about this experience in her famous book, *The Hiding Place*. The ten Booms acted out of Christian conviction. Corrie, her sister and their parents were subsequently sent to a concentration camp; all but Corrie perished.

The vast majority of anti-Semitic expressions in the past 2,000 years have not been motivated by Christian churches or theologies but by the mindless rejection of "strangers" – those who are different – which is inherent in fallen human nature. If anything, anti-Semitism has been opposed, or at least moderated, by the Christian Church throughout history. It is not necessarily Christians who unthinkingly cry "Christ-killers" but, rather, pagan Westerners acting out of common ignorance.

WITCH-HUNTING

It is fascinating that the New Testament does not mention witches. From time to time demons are cast out by Jesus and the apostles, but the person who is possessed is never blamed and is always an object of compassion. Witch-hunting – and certainly witch burning – is clearly at cross-purposes with New Testament teachings. New Testament Christians believed in the principle, "Whatever is born of God overcomes the world: and this is the victory that overcomes the world, even our faith."[13] The world is the domain of Satan, but Christians have nothing to fear from it.

Throughout the New Testament we're taught that Christians can have confidence in their power over the forces of evil because of the presence of Christ.

So, even though some Christians practiced it, witch-hunts and witch burnings are unknown in and contrary to the New Testament. They are not Christian in any sense, even when undertaken by Christians. They are, rather, a throwback to European paganism and folk religion that predates the introduction of Christianity to Europe and its importation to America.

So, what happened?

The era in which witchcraft prospered in Europe, and later in America, began around 1450, but was concentrated in the years 1590 to 1650. It is estimated that the number of men and women who were executed as witches in Europe during that period was about 60,000 – a significant number.[14]

The persistence of witchcraft trials was linked to the persistence of magic: "People kept doing magic and the Church kept misinterpreting it as Satanism."[15] The classical world still influenced the Christian world during the three centuries of the witch trials. And the classical world was a magical world – a world of astrology, amulets, charms and curses.[16] When the Church came to power, belief in magic was everywhere and took a long time to extinguish. Charges of witchcraft seldom originated from a priest or minister. Strangely, intellectuals are found among those who believed in persecuting witches. The distinguished scientist Robert Boyle (1627-1690), for example, encouraged witch-hunts. Thomas Hobbes (1599-1679), the famous British philosopher, dismissed all religion as "credulity" but believed that "witches … are justly punished."[17]

The most important factor in solving the mystery of witch-hunts is understanding that their growth coincided with the intense religious conflict and turmoil preceding, leading up to and including the Protestant Reformation. One theory asserts that they were "collateral damage" during a time of heresy trials, in the same way that anti-Semitism was "collateral damage" at the time of the Crusades. The broad impact of religious conflict during the Reformation was, regrettably, less tolerance, in general, for non-conformity.

Those accused of witchcraft were often nonconformist in the sense of being community misfits, people whose behavior was, in some sense, strange. Such people would be arrested, tortured, forced to confess (to end the torture) and forced to implicate others. Those implicated people, in turn, would be arrested until everyone who could not be vouched for by others had been tortured, convicted and, often, executed. Only then would the rash of trials in a particular city or village end. Witch "crazes," therefore, tended to cease after one person in 20 had been killed and the whole community began to feel at risk.[18]

When the period of religious conflict due to heresy trials ceased, witch-hunting also ceased. So, in 1648, when the Peace of Westphalia was signed, the treaty agreed upon boundaries between Catholics and Protestants – who, without boundaries, had tended to try each other for heresy – and provided for the toleration of Protestant worship in Catholic territories and vice versa. It is not coincidental that this also marked the date of the end of widespread witch-hunting, subsequently reduced to only scattered trials.

Though the witch-hunts, trials and executions took place in a time of great religious tension, the time of the Reformation and consequent conflict between Protestants and Catholics, there is no Biblical basis for them and so they fall under the category, mentioned at the beginning of this chapter, of Christians acting in un-Christian ways. In fact, the witch-hunt crazes in many localities were ended when respected clergy stepped in to end them or wrote to expose them.[19]

THE SPANISH INQUISITION

The Inquisition (1540-1700) occurred in the intense period of religious conflict immediately preceding the Reformation. It can also be considered related to the religious turmoil of that Protestant-Catholic conflict.

In Spain, as in other areas, the Inquisition, or panel of ecclesiastical judges, had jurisdiction over such offenses as heresy, blasphemy, superstition, witchcraft and sexual irregularities.[20] One of the least known facts of the Spanish Inquisition is that only 1.8 percent of those brought to trial were executed.[21]

The tragedy of the Inquisition is that it took place at all. Its clerical leaders had the authority to exact penalties and proclaim sentences – even execution. In the broad sense, it was not just Catholic. Even the Puritans had heresy trials, as did John Calvin in Zurich and the English Protestants in the British Isles.

All of this, however, was quite beyond the bounds of Biblical

Christianity. In the New Testament church, the only significant penalty meted out by man was excommunication – exclusion from the fellowship of believers. Moreover, the Apostle Paul makes it plain in the Corinthian letters that the purpose of such exclusion is to lead to repentance and re-inclusion.

The whole concept of the church sentencing people to torture, as was true at times during the Spanish Inquisition, is completely outside the bounds of Biblical Christianity and is another example of the truths mentioned above:

• Not all those who claim to be Christians are.

• Not all Christians act like Christians should.

CONCLUSION

In summary, the world that God has created, as pictured in Christianity, is a world peopled with people who possess free will. The question dealt with in this chapter is not whether those who claim to be the Church ever fail, but whether Biblical Christianity, as a whole, has been the cause of those failures. Clearly, it is not Biblical Christianity, but a perversion of it or forces outside of it, that produced much of the suffering and madness that is often attributed to Christianity.

Chapter Nine

Conclusion

The time has come to step back, get some perspective and ask what all this adds up to. We have discussed six great ideas of the Christian faith. What is the point of this exercise? Here they are in summary:

- "The world is comprehensible because it existed first in the mind and plan of God." From that revolutionary idea, which desacralized nature, science arose.

- "Truth is one because all truth is God's truth." From that idea, which unified knowledge and made possible freedom of inquiry without fear, the university arose.

- "All human beings are created in the image of God." Thus, the institution of slavery fell in Christendom and throughout the world, as other cultures were shamed into abolishing it by the example of the Christian West.

- "Men and women are created equal." Feminism, even in its most extreme forms, owes its birth to the Christian faith and to the Bible, the source of this great idea.

- "Every human being is a sinner; every human being is loved by God." What a profound basis for a civil government! And what an amazing government that idea produced in America.

- "We cannot be good without God." This may be the most controversial of all the great ideas contributed by the Christian faith, but it is certainly Biblical.

THE DIFFERENCE

The rise of science. The idea of the university. The abolition of slavery, culminating in the modern civil rights movement. The emancipation of women. American political theory. Christian morality and consequent humanitarianism. What a legacy all of this is! Indeed, a two-thousand-year-old legacy.

What would life be like without it?

There would be technology, but not science. Only in the Christian West did science develop. Technology had gone about as far as it could go by the year 1500. Then came science. Without it, we all would be experiencing first-hand what it was like to live before 1500.

There would be no universities, no learning about everything "all together." Instead, every level of education from kindergarten through graduate school would be done in competing sectarian "pockets" of learning. The concept of the *general* advancement of knowledge would be unknown. Parochial indoctrination would be the rule.

Every culture that could afford it would have at least some slaves. There is little if any reason to believe that that cultural commonality, which existed prior to the ascendancy of Christianity, would have been abolished without Christianity. It wouldn't have happened in Islam. It wouldn't have happened in Hinduism. It wouldn't have happened in American Indian culture. Where would it have happened? Where would the idea that slavery is flat-out wrong have come from, if not from the Christian faith?

Throughout the world, women would still be second-class citizens. Their physical weakness, childbearing inevitabilities and maternal responsibilities would have continually kept them dependent upon men and, therefore, inferior to their male counterparts. Without the Judeo-Christian idea that men and women were created equal by God, how would the idea of equality have crept into culture?

Even though the idea of freedom is deeply ingrained in the human heart, the idea of tyranny is, as well. In many ways dictatorships, oligarchies and anarchies (feudal societies, for example) have always been the preferred form of human government. Even Greek democracy was very different than ours. Do we really think that American democracy – based on the consent of the governed, grounded in an ethic of love and a recognition of the problem of sin – would have arisen apart from Christianity?

And why do most people in America today think polygamy and bribery and greed are wrong? If it were not for the Christian moral values at the historical root of this culture, do we really believe the "domestic tranquility" we enjoy as a nation would exist at the level it does?

To many, the evidence for this Christian legacy may be more convincing in some instances than in others, but the overall argument is overwhelming. The cumulative effect of a rock avalanche is much more convincing than just one rock. The great beneficial influence of Christianity on Western culture and the cultures of the world is simply unmistakable.

CHRISTIANITY AND TWO CENTURIES OF AMERICAN HISTORY

Another way to assess this legacy is to glance briefly at the history of the United States and ask some questions.

Since the founding of the country, the United States of America has faced a number of issues which have dominated its history and in which the Christian faith has played a salutary role. What might have been if not for the positive influence of Christianity in our national life?

The issue that dominated American life from the adoption of the Constitution to the middle of the 19th century was, of course, slavery. That issue was settled in 1865 by the bloodbath of the Civil War. As demonstrated, the Christian faith was a leading influence in the anti-slavery movement, both here and around the world. What would our history have been like without Christianity?

The next great issue, dominating the national landscape from 1865 to 1920, was the women's suffrage movement, with the gradual emancipation of women as its basis. The bookends of this period were the 14th and 19th amendments to the U.S. Constitution. The 14th Amendment, passed in 1865, gave the right to vote to freed male slaves by giving that right to every male citizen over 21 years of age. The long-established custom of limiting the vote to males was placed, perhaps inadvertently, into the Constitution for the first time. The 19th Amendment, passed 55 years later, explicitly gave the vote to women for the first time. The Christian faith played a major role, first, in the education of women and then, in the women's suffrage movement itself. What would our history have been like without that faith?

From 1930 to 1940, the Great Depression overwhelmed America.

There is, and has been, a common opinion that poverty begets crime, but the anomaly of the Depression was that crime did not happen. There was essentially no increase in crime during that time. What was it that kept the law-abiding citizens of the country from turning to crime under the pressure of this poverty? Why were we a law-abiding country in the first place? The Founders had very definite ideas about that question. Were they right? What would the period of the Great Depression have been like without the basis of morality provided by the Christian faith?

From 1940 to 1945, the nation lost hundreds of thousands of its sons during the war in Europe, a war that posed no immediate threat to America and which, it could be argued – and has been argued – we never should have entered. For largely altruistic reasons, however, the supporters of isolationism lost the debate and this nation made the decision to help rescue Europe from Hitler.

After the war was over, again for altruistic reasons, this nation decided to rebuild Europe, including Germany, through the Marshall Plan, and Japan as well. From that conflict and from the Marshall Plan, the United States gained nothing for itself except a safer world. Could it be that that altruism and that rescue, which cost this nation so dearly, were motivated by the moral influence of the Christian faith?

Then the nation plunged into the Cold War. Communism never gained a significant foothold in this country, in part because it is atheistic. Americans were not about to be taken in by a political scheme that had, at its heart, the doctrine that religion is the opiate of the masses. Could it be that the Christian faith had something to do with the fact that communism was a non-starter here at home? Toward the end of the century, we finally won the Cold War and again set about helping our former enemies rebuild.

Finally, on September 11, 2001, the challenge of Islamic terrorism hit us hard. Since that time this country, again at the cost of many lives, has made the decision not to be isolationist in the face of the worldwide challenge of terrorism. It chose, instead, to bring freedom and democracy, first to Afghanistan and then to Iraq, in the hope that the dictatorships of the Middle East, which first birthed Islamic terrorism, would find that the freedom seeded in these two countries can thrive in that area of the world. The jury is still out on this gamble, of course, but the vision of democracy and freedom on which it is based is the same one on which this nation was founded. Could it be that, ultimately, it springs from the same root – the Christian faith?

THE QUESTION OF TRUTH

Ultimately, these six great ideas raise a few questions: What does this legacy say about the truth and reality of the Christian faith? Does the Christian faith contain the answer to the mystery of life and human existence? Is this legacy, in effect, evidence that may lead us to God?

Now, I know that even to speak of truth in this way goes against the grain of today's American culture. Doesn't everyone have his or her own truth? Doesn't *Jesus Christ Superstar* say, "We all have our truths, but are mine the same as yours?" implying that the answer is "No," and that's just fine? Isn't Hinduism just as true as Christianity, which is just as true as Scientology, which is just as true as Islam, which is just as true as witchcraft – and on and on? Aren't all religions equally true, and don't they just represent different roads up the same mountain? As the old poem says:

Ten thousand paths may lead to God.
What right is mine to say
That he who fails to walk with me
Has missed the only way?

What right of mine to arrogate
Such grasp of finite mind
And boast while others vainly seek
The God I seek and find.
How could the God I love and trust
Point out to only me
The way which travel all men must
To life eternally?

I'm not so wise that He denies
The light to all save me,
While other hearts as true as mine
He loves with less degree.

So if the path we tread should lead
Where bright Cathedrals rise,
Or weathered church or rustic shrine
Point upward to the skies,

> Each sincere traveler will arrive
> Where lights of welcome shine
> And myriads will be there who walked
> A different path than mine.[1]

To put this illustration another way, many people liken different understandings of God to three blind men describing an elephant as they touch it. One touches the elephant's tusk and says, "An elephant is smooth and very hard." Another touches the elephant's trunk and says, "An elephant is long and curved with a nose at the end." Still another touches the side of the elephant and says, "An elephant is huge with very rough skin."

So, the illustration says, many people in different religions see God differently, but it is all one and the same God. The problem with this illustration is that an elephant is not everything. It is one thing. There are many things that it is not. There is one truth about what a real elephant is, and it is one non-contradictory truth. So, also, there is one truth about who the real God is and is not. There are not 10,000 equally true views of God.

People who think that one religion is as true as another are really atheists who believe that all religions are fairy tales, so it doesn't really matter what you believe. There cannot be 60 different, contradictory answers to the mystery of life.

To use a scientific analogy, either we live in an expanding universe that began with a "Big Bang," or we don't. It is nonsense to say, "That's true for you, but not for me." Likewise, if I say it is God the Creator of all who lit the initial fuse of the Big Bang, and you say He didn't, we can't both be right. If I say Jesus was God's Son who came down from heaven to save the world, and you say He wasn't and didn't, we can't both be right.

As we board a plane and the flight attendant says, "This plane is going to Burlington, Vermont," and we reply, "I thought it was going to Portland, Maine," it doesn't make sense for her to reply, "Oh well, it doesn't matter." It does matter. And so does the truth about our existence and where we have come from and where we are going and whether there is a God and whether there is life after death. We may not know that truth, but we know that it exists. And when a child asks, "How did we really get here, Daddy?" we'd better not say, "There are lots of answers to that question and they are all true!"

It has been said that life is like being on a sailing ship on which no one knows either the port of origin or the port of destination. We may not know, but we human beings on this earth came from somewhere, and we are going somewhere. The explanation of where we came from may be "chance" – we come from chance happenings. The explanation of where we are going may be "the heat death of the universe" – and the whole universe ultimately will just burn out. But there is an answer to the mystery of where we come from and where we are going.

The question is, "Is this wonderful legacy of the Christian faith one piece of evidence for the truth of Christianity?" There is other evidence, of course: the evidence of beauty, love, nature and prophecy; the life of Jesus; the evidence of and for His Resurrection; the birth of the Christian Church against all odds; the evidence of experience.

WORLDVIEWS

As was described in the first chapter, all people have a worldview – an understanding of the mystery of life by which they live. A worldview is simply a set of assumptions about the nature and meaning of life. We may not be aware of our assumptions, but they exist. And we live by them. They shape the nature and meaning of life for us. That's what worldviews do.

Since worldviews can't be proven, they are all a rough combination of evidence and faith. Are you an atheist? Well, you have some evidence for that worldview – and a whole lot of faith because you certainly can't prove it. Are you a Christian? Well, you have some evidence and some faith. It is naïve at best and stupid at worst to say of world religions that "these rival belief systems are equally uncontaminated by evidence."[2] Or to say, "Faith – blind, deaf, dumb, and unreasoned – threatens our very existence."[3] No one has a worldview based only on faith; everyone has *some* evidence, however inadequate it may be. And no one has a worldview based only on evidence; everyone has some faith, as well. If there were no faith involved, the right worldview could be proven to all and that would be the end of it. Need I point out that that hasn't happened yet?

So, I ask again: "What does this legacy of the Christian faith say about the truth of Christianity? Is it evidence for the truth of the Christian worldview?" "Does it tend to make us say, 'If I am happy to enjoy all these benefits that have come to the world through the Christian faith, maybe the time has come to consider whether or not the Christian faith itself is true and is the revelation of the God who created everything?'"

Another way to put it is, "If the optimism I feel about life really comes to me from the Christian faith, maybe I should consider making that faith my own." That faith, quite simply, is faith in the God of creation, who "so loved the world that He gave His only Son, that whoever believes in Him should not perish but have eternal life."[4] Hundreds of passages in the New Testament say the same thing in just slightly different words.[5]

The Christian faith says we are all "perishing," running away from the God who made us and loves us, living our lives independent of Him. But God has provided a way back to Himself in "giving" His "only Son" for the world. Those who turn back and "believe in" His Son find fellowship with God, become His children and inherit "eternal life" in His presence. All we have to do is say, "Yes," make a decision to believe and then follow that new worldview with our lives – devoting ourselves to the reading of the Bible to learn more about God; to the fellowship of other Christians to be encouraged in our life with God; to the worship of the God who made us and loves us, rejoicing in who He is; and to conversation with Him in prayer, sharing our life with God.[6]

The wonderful legacy of the Christian faith points not only to the truth of the faith, but also to the joy of it. It is the best and the most fulfilling of all possible lives. It is a hopeful life. As the Apostle Paul, focusing on the word "hope," said,

> May the God of hope fill you with all joy and peace in believing,
> so that by the power of the Holy Spirit you may abound in hope.[7]

'THE STORY OF THE BIBLE'

The Bible is a love letter from God to all humankind. It is about God's love for us. It is a story told through a recounting of God's interactions with people, beginning with Adam and Eve and the Fall of Man.

At the beginning, in Genesis 3, man turned away from God, who made him for fellowship with Himself. Man, instead, decided to live independently of God. And so, the Bible begins with man's chief problem: the desire to live without God, doing as he pleases, using his God-given gift of free will without realizing that his own happiness lies in fellowship with God.

The same independence that led man to break his relationship with God then leads him to break his relationship with his fellow human beings. Thus, the Bible sees a very close relationship between man's failure to love God with all his heart and his failure to love his neighbor as himself. These are the two great commands man has broken and which have thereby changed human life in the most dreadful way. These are the reasons for war, pride, selfishness, envy, deceit and hate.

But God did not give up on man. He revealed himself to a man named Abraham, God's beachhead in a lost and fallen world. God had a plan to win human beings back to Himself, a plan that began with His revelation to one man. God promised Abraham that if he would follow Him, God would bless him, make him a blessing to the whole world and give him more descendants than the stars of the heavens. God took care of Abraham, even though Abraham failed God many times. Abraham had children who in turn had children from generation to generation. Thus, the nation of Israel came into being, a nation that knew God's love, His commandments for our welfare and His forgiveness. The forgiveness was expressed through animal sacrifices, as a way of saying that God's forgiveness is costly. They pointed toward the ultimate sacrifice that was to be His Son, Jesus Christ.

The history of Israel is a history of blessing and punishment, of faithfulness and fallenness, of correction and promise. God sent many prophets to Israel to warn the people when they strayed and to lead them back to Himself. They were to be His first family, commissioned to carry His love and forgiveness to every nation. They predicted that God would one day send the Savior, His only Son, to die, that the world might be forgiven. He died as the ultimate sacrifice for sin and then was raised from the dead to show that victory over man's sinfulness had been accomplished.

The great turning point in history, toward which the prophets looked and to which Christians look back, was the coming of His Son to give His life as a ransom for many. That Son was Jesus, the God-Man, fully God and yet fully human. Jesus was God Himself entering the world He had made in order to rescue it from its own evil and the death to which evil inevitably leads. Death in this sense is spiritual. It is eternal separation from God. It is inherent in evil and is the natural result of evil. It is to be independent from God – not just for a while, but forever. That is what God, at all costs, was seeking to avoid. That is why He gave His Son for us: to save us from eternal separation from Himself.

The New Testament is the story of Jesus' life, death and resurrection and how the message of God's love began to spread throughout the world through His people – the Church. The Church is people who have given themselves back to God so that the separation can end. This was all made possible by God through Jesus, the ultimate expression of God's love. Through Him, those who believe in Him and want forgiveness become members of God's family and begin to see their lives transformed here and now by Jesus, who lives within them through His Spirit. They are promised that nothing will ever separate them from God's love.

Christians are not perfect, but they are being transformed in spite of the fact that they continue to sin. They simply repent, get back on their feet, brush themselves off and continue their journey with Jesus, which, at death or at the coming again of Jesus to the earth in His glory, ends in life forever in His presence – the great hope to which every Christian looks. That promise of glory will be fulfilled in everlasting communion with God.

In the meantime, while life continues here on earth, God blesses those who love Him with love, joy and peace. His promise is that He shows mercy to thousands of those who love Him and keep His commandments. Thus, wherever they are, Christians bring blessings not only to themselves, but also to those around them. And those blessings include the body of great ideas about which this book has been written.

Appendix I

'St. Patrick's Breastplate'

I arise today
Through a mighty strength, the invocation of the Trinity,
Through belief in the threeness,
Through confession of the oneness
Of the Creator of Creation. ...

I arise today
Through the strength of Christ's birth with His baptism,
Through the strength of His crucifixion with His burial,
Through the strength of His resurrection with His ascension,
Through the strength of His descent for the judgment of Doom.

I arise today
Through the strength of the love of Cherubim,
In obedience of angels,
In the service of archangels,
In hope of resurrection to meet with reward,
In prayers of patriarchs,
In predictions of prophets,
In preaching of apostles,
In faith of confessors,
In innocence of holy virgins,

In deeds of righteous men.
I arise today
Through the strength of heaven:
Light of sun,
Radiance of moon,
Splendor of fire,
Speed of lightning,
Swiftness of wind,
Depth of sea,
Stability of earth,
Firmness of rock.

I arise today
Through God's strength to pilot me:
God's might to uphold me,
God's wisdom to guide me,
God's eye to look before me,
God's ear to hear me,
God's word to speak for me,
God's hand to guard me,
God's way to lie before me,
God's shield to protect me,
God's host to save me
From snares of devils,
From temptations of vices,
From everyone who shall wish me ill,
Afar and anear,
Alone and in multitude.

I summon today all these powers between me and those evils,
Against every cruel merciless power that may oppose my body and soul
Against incantations of false prophets
Against black laws of pagandom,
Against false laws of heretics,
Against craft of idolatry,
Against spells of witches and smiths and wizards,
Against every knowledge that corrupts man's body and soul.

Christ to shield me today
Against poison, against burning,
Against drowning, against wounding
So that there may come to me abundance of reward.
Christ with me, Christ before me, Christ behind me,
Christ in me, Christ beneath me, Christ above me,
Christ on my right, Christ on my left,
Christ when I lie down, Christ when I sit down, Christ
     when I arise,
Christ in the heart of every man who thinks of me,
Christ in the mouth of everyone who speaks of me,
Christ in every eye that sees me,
Christ in every ear that hears me.

I arise today
Through a mighty strength, the invocation of the Trinity,
Through belief in the threeness,
Through confession of the oneness,
Of the Creator of Creation.

Thomas Cahill, *How the Irish Saved Civilization: The Untold Story of Ireland's Heroic Role from the Fall of Rome to the Rise of Medieval Europe* (Doubleday: Garden City, N.Y.; 1995), pp. 116-9.

APPENDIX II

Group Study Guide:
FORGOTTEN FOUNDATION

Week One ('The Introduction')

Read Genesis 1-3.

1. List as many of the "great ideas" (great facts about the nature of existence and of human life) as you can from these chapters. Don't stop until you have listed at least five from each chapter. Divide into three groups, with each assigned a chapter. Then come together and read each chapter aloud. List the great ideas for each chapter. Discuss.

2. How have these ideas influenced the culture we live in today? Where do you see them?

3. To what extent are these ideas acknowledged as foundational to our culture today, or have they been forgotten? Pick one idea and talk about it in these terms.

4. What difference do any of these ideas make in the way you ...
    ... see life?
    ... make decisions at work?

Week Two (Chapter One: 'Worldviews')

Read Hebrews 11:1-16.

1. If a worldview means what we think is the nature and meaning of life – or who we are, where we came from and where we are going – what is your worldview?

2. How fundamental is your worldview to your mood, your understanding of family life, your performance at work?

3. What are examples of other worldviews that are "out there?"

4. What would you imagine is the worldview of an atheistic scientist?
    Of a rapper in an inner-city gang?
    Of a traditional American Indian?
    Of a Communist?

5. What role does faith play in your worldview? In all worldviews?

6. What role does faith play in the worldview of the folks mentioned in Hebrews 11:1-16?

Week Three (Chapter Two: 'Science')

Read Genesis 1 and 2 again.

1. Science is founded on the great ideas of the Christian faith, which say that the world makes sense because it existed first in the mind and plan of God. The first scientists spoke of God's two books, the Book of his Word, the Bible, and the Book of his Works, the Creation. They believed that both reveal His glory. Read Psalm 19. How does it reflect these two themes?

2. Animism, the belief that the world is inhabited by the spirits of mountains, streams and lakes, sees all of nature as alive with different spirits. In animism, all of nature is "inhabited" and "sacred." How would this worldview inhibit the rise of science?

3. Hindus believe that the material world is an illusion. How would this worldview inhibit the rise of science?

4. Classical Greeks believed that the physical world was "earthly" and unworthy of the attention of philosophers. How would this worldview inhibit the rise of science?

5. Islam sees God as doing whatever He wants with nature at any time, like a puppet master pulling strings. The saying is, "It is the will of Allah," whether speaking of a nice day or of a hurricane. How would this worldview inhibit the rise of science?

6. Read Genesis 1:29. How does this verse encourage science?

7. Read Genesis 2:19. How does this verse encourage science?

8. Read Romans 1:19-21. In what sense is the creation an evidence of God?

9. Do you commonly see God's glory in nature? Explain.

Week Four (Chapter Three: 'The Idea of the University')

1. The word "university" means "all together." Historically, the concept of the university comes from the great idea that truth is one because all truth is God's truth. To what extent do universities today focus on diversity of knowledge (lots of unrelated truths) or unity of knowledge (lots of related truths)?

2. In John 8:31, 32, Jesus speaks about knowing the truth. What does He say is the key to knowing the truth?

3. In what sense does knowing the truth make us free?

4. Why, would you guess, has the Christian faith historically had the understanding that no truth is to be feared and that all truth is worthy of study?

5. Can you think of any examples of the fear of truth ...
        ... in Islam?
        ... in the Jehovah's Witnesses?
        ... among secularists?

6. To what extent are universities today genuinely open to the pursuit of truth …

    … concerning Christianity?

    … concerning anything?

7. To what extent are your friends open to the pursuit of truth?

8. Why are people sometimes open and sometimes closed to the pursuit of truth?

9. What can we do to encourage this openness to seek the truth – at the center of which is God Himself?

Week Five (Chapter Four: 'The Abolition of Slavery')

1. As an introduction to this topic, read aloud the questions and answers on pages 53-55 in this book.

2. The great idea of the Christian faith that caused the downfall of slavery is the idea that there is an inherent dignity in every human being because all human beings are created in the image of God. Read Genesis 1:26, 27 and Matthew 22:36-38.What do these passages imply about slavery?

3. Many passages in the New Testament deal with the issue of slavery. Divide them among members of the group. Look them up individually and then discuss them as a group: Ephesians 6:9; Colossians 4:1; Acts 10:34; Romans 2:11; Colossians 3:25; Galatians 3:27, 28; Colossians 3:29; Philemon 10-16; and Matthew 28:19.

4. Can you come to a coherent conclusion from these passages of what the New Testament attitude was toward slavery?

5. What does this conclusion say about our own attitude toward people today?

Week Six (Chapter Five: 'The Emancipation of Women')

1. It is a great idea of the Christian faith that men and women are created equal. Read and discuss Genesis 1:27, 28. This is where it all

begins in the Bible.

2. Women were very important in the teaching of Jesus. Look up and discuss these passages: Mark 15:41; Mark 15:47; Mark 16:1; Mark 16:6; John 20:14-17.

3. Women were also prominent in Jesus' preaching and healing. What passages can you think of in this regard?

4. Read Matthew 22:30. What does this verse and passage have to say about male/female equality? What about I Peter 3:7?

5. Paul is often mischaracterized as being "against" women, but what does Galatians 3:27, 28 say about that subject?

6. Look up these passages about the role of women in the New Testament Church: Acts 18:26; Romans 16:1, 4; I Corinthians 11:5; I Corinthians 14:33-35 and Philippians 4:3. What do these passages add to the picture of the role and nature of women in the New Testament?

7. In your experience, how are women treated in non-Christian cultural settings? Give examples.

8. How is God calling each of us to honor women today?

Week Seven (Chapter 6: 'American Democracy')

1. One of the great ideas of the Christian faith upon which American democracy is based is that every human being is a sinner and, at the same time, loved by God. Where do you see this in our founding documents (i.e., the Declaration of Independence, the Constitution, the Bill of Rights)?

2. How do you find this reflected in John 3:16, Romans 3:23-25 and Romans 5:8?

3. In your recollection of the history of the Pilgrims and Plymouth Plantation, how do you see this lived out?

4. The Founders saw this as a Christian nation. Many today see it as a

secular nation. What is lost or gained either way?

5. How can the Christian faith continue to influence this nation for good?

6. What is your role and the role of your church in that influence?

Week Eight (Chapter 7: 'Moral Values')

1. The last of the six great ideas of the Christian faith that were crucial to the development of modern civilization – and the most controversial one – is that we cannot be good without God. In what sense do you think this is true or not true?

2. What does Peter say is the core value of Christian conduct in I Peter 1:13-16?

3. In Matthew 22:35-40, what is the relationship between the first and second commandments? How closely are they connected?

4. Can Christian morality survive apart from Christianity? Discuss at length.

5. How can we preserve the moral fiber of the nation?

Appendix III

Notes

The Introduction

1. Colleen Carroll Campbell, "Jesus Christ Superfluous," *First Things*, April 2005, 45.

2. George Will, Speech delivered at Hillsdale College and printed in *Imprimis*, Volume 34, Number 9, Sept. 2005, 1.

3. Thomas Jefferson, *Declaration of Independence*, 1776.

Chapter One

1. Huston Smith, *Why Religion Matters, the Fate of the Human Spirit in an Age of Disbelief* (New York: HarperCollins, 2001) 11.

2. Ibid., 25.

3. Ibid., 21.

4. Robert N. Bellah, *Habits of the Heart: Individualism and Commitment in American Life* (New York: Harper and Row, 1985) 221.

5. Isaiah 44:13-19 (NIV).

6. Philip J. Sampson, *Six Modern Myths about Christianity and Western Civilization* (Wheaton, Ill.: InterVarsity Press, 2000) 158.

7.   James W. Sire, *The Universe Next Door* (Wheaton, Ill.: InterVarsity Press, 1988) 149.

8.   Rodney Stark, *For the Glory of God: How Monotheism Led to Science, Witch-hunts, and the End of Slavery* (Princeton, N.J.: Princeton University Press, 2003) 6.

9.   This cultural foreignness is much deeper than the "burkah" (head covering) worn by Muslim women and the five-times-daily prayers practiced by Muslim men, interrupting work schedules. Even a cursory reading of the Koran reveals other cultural problems:
     * sanction of religious war: "Fight against them until idolatry is no more and God's religion reigns supreme." 2:193
     * "fight for the cause of God," 4:75 (a command repeated hundreds of times in the Koran).
     * "slay the idolaters wherever you find them." 9:5
     * "Believers, make war on the infidels who dwell around you." 9:121
     * the general status of women: "men have a status above women." 2:226
     * "Men have authority over women because God made one superior to the other. ... As for those [women] from whom you fear disobedience ... beat them." 4:34
     * cultural exclusivism or ghettoism: "Believers, do not make friends with any but your own people." 3:118
     * acceptance of polygamy. 4:126
     * "wives and slave girls." 23:5
     * draconian punishments: "As for the man or woman who is guilty of theft, cut off their hands."
     * the multiple virgins with which fighters for Islam are rewarded when they enter heaven. 32:48 (and more than a dozen additional references).

10.   Smith, *Why Religion Matters*, 60.

11.   Ibid., 183-4.

12.   Richard Dawkins, *A Devil's Chaplain: Reflections on Hope, Lies, Science and Love* (Boston: Houghton Mifflin, 2003) 242-8.

13.   Judith Newman, "Blind Faith: Is There a God?" *Ladies Home Journal*, December 2003, 40-2.

14.   Howard Mumma, *Albert Camus and the Minister* (Orleans, Mass.: Paraclete Press, 2000) 86-90.

15.   I John 1:5 (RSV).

16.   I John 4:8 (RSV).

17. I Corinthians 13:13 (RSV).

18. Thomas Cahill, *How the Irish Saved Civilization: The Untold Story of Ireland's Heroic Role from the Fall of Rome to the Rise of Medieval Europe* (New York: Doubleday, 1995) 116-9.

19. Sam Harris, *The End of Faith: Religion, Terror and the Future of Reason* (New York: Norton, 2004) 12.

20. Ibid., 15.

21. Ibid., 20.

22. Sean Hannity, *Deliver Us From Evil: Defeating Terrorism, Despotism and Liberalism* (New York: HarperCollins, 2004) 2.

23. Ibid., 3.

24. Ann Coulter, *How to Talk with a Liberal: The World According to Ann Coulter* (New York: Crown Forum, 2004) 162.

25. Don Oberdorfer, *Princeton University: The First 250 Years* (Trustees of Princeton University, 1995) 10.

CHAPTER TWO

1. Stark, *For the Glory of God*, 388.

2. Ibid., 122. Further, Stark comments, "The Venerable Bede (c. 673-720) taught that the world was round, as did Bishop Virgilius of Salzburg (c. 720-784), Hildegaard of Bingen (c. 1099-1179) and Thomas Aquinas (c. 1224-1274) and all four ended up as saints."

3. Ibid., 120.

4. Ibid., 121.

5. Ibid., 123. Of course, there was astrology in ancient times, but not the science, astronomy. There also was mathematics, geometry, iron, bronze and different sorts of technology. But none of these was "science" as it has been defined for the past four centuries.

6. Ibid., 124-5.

7. Albert Einstein exhibit at the San Diego Science Museum, Spring 2005.

8. Genesis 1:1, 31a (RSV).

9. Psalms 119:1 (RSV).

10. Genesis 1:29 (RSV).

11. Genesis 2:19 (RSV).

12. These assumptions are a summary of those discussed by Nancy R. Pearcey and Charles B. Thaxton in their book, *The Soul of Science: Christian Faith and Natural Philosophy* (New York: Crossway Books, 1994) 22-37.

13. Ibid., 23.

14. Ibid., 24.

15. 1Ibid., 24.

16. Ibid., 25.

17. Ibid., 25.

18. Ibid., 27.

19. Stark, *For the Glory of God*, 163.

20. Avery Cardinal Dulles, "The Deist Minimum," *First Things*, January 2005.

21. Stark, *For the Glory of God*, 135-6. "Scholastic" is an adjective referring to scholars of the Middle Ages influenced by Aristotle and the Christian tradition.

22. Pearcey and Thaxton, *The Soul of Science*, 40.

23. Ibid., 40.

24. Stark, *For the Glory of God*, 175.

25. George M. Marsden, *The Soul of the American University: From Protestant Establishment to Established Non-belief* (New York: Oxford University Press, 1994) 197.

26. Stark, *For the Glory of God*, 176-7.

27. Ibid., 185.

28. Ibid., 190-2.

29. Bill Bryson, *A Short History of Nearly Everything* (New York: Broadway Books, 2003) 1-2.

30. Ibid., 2-3.

31. Stark, *For the Glory of God*, 184.

32. Romans 1:19-21 (RSV).

33. Because the roots of science lie primarily in the Old Testament, it is important to include the beliefs of Jews as well as Christians in the characterization of this legacy.

34. Stark, *For the Glory of God*, 154-5. Although similar ideas concerning the sovereignty of God and His ability to intervene in nature exist in Christianity (e.g., Moses and the Israelites crossing the Red Sea), the picture of nature operating according to natural God-given laws found in Genesis 1 is not found in Islam. Suffice it to say that no comparable "major theological bloc" ever developed in Christianity.

CHAPTER THREE

1. Tom Wolfe, *I Am Charlotte Simmons* (New York: Farrar, Strauss and Giroux, 2004) 3-4.

2. Ibid., 285.

3. Ibid., 285.

4. *Webster's New World Dictionary* (New York: Simon and Schuster, 1988).

5. John 8:31, 32 (RSV).

6. Stark, *For the Glory of God*, 147.

7. Marsden, *The Soul of the American University*, 50.

8. Richard John Neuhaus, "The Public Square," *First Things*, April 2005, 66.

9. Stephen Hawking, *A Brief History of Time* (New York: Bantam Books, 1988), 12.

10. Romans 1:19-33 (RSV).

11. Romans 2:8-16 (RSV).

12. Cahill, *How the Irish Saved Civilization*, 191-5.

13. Ibid., 191-5.

14. Stark, *For the Glory of God*, 142.

15. Ibid., 143.

16. Ibid., 144.

17. Marsden, *The Soul of the American University*, 46.

18. Ibid., 49.

19. Ibid., 33.

20. Ibid., 33.

21. Ibid., 53.

22. Ibid., 22.

23. Ibid., 57.

24. Ibid., 219.

25. In 2002, Steven Pinker, a professor at the Massachusetts Institute of Technology, published a book titled *The Blank Slate, the Modern Denial of Human Nature* (Penguin), in which he asserted that in the great nature-nurture debate in psychology today, the answer is that *both* play a prominent role in mental development. We are not merely "blank slates," as every parent instinctively knows.

26. Quoted in the *Wall Street Journal*'s lead editorial, "Straight Talking," March 4, 2005, p. W13.

27. Allan Bloom, *The Closing of the American Mind: How Higher Education Has Failed Democracy and Impoverished the Souls of Today's Students* (New York: Simon and Schuster, 1987) 25.

28. Anyone who is widely read on homosexuality is aware of these myths. The best single source of information on them of which I am aware is a book by Robert Gagnon, *The Bible and Homosexual Practice* (Nashville, Tenn: Abingdon Press, 2001), which has an excellent section on the current science on the subject, pp. 395-430.

29. Robert Spitzer, *Archives of Sexual Behavior*, Volume 32, No. 5, October 2003, 403-17.

30. Thomas E. Schmidt, *Straight and Narrow: Compassion and Clarity in the Homosexuality Debate* (Wheaton, Ill.: InterVarsity Press, 1995), 127. Schmidt summarizes the problems as follows: The most poignant way to summarize the barrage of statistics and descriptions in this chapter is to translate them into an illustration. Suppose you were to move into a large house in San Francisco with a group of 10 randomly selected homosexual men in their mid-thirties. According to the most recent research from scientific sources, whose authors are without exception either neutral or positive in their assessment of homosexual behavior, and with the use of lower numbers where statistics differ, the relational and physical health of the group would look like this. Four of the 10 men currently are in relationships, but only one of those is faithful to his partner and he will not be within a year. Four have never had a relationship that lasted more than a year, and only one has had a relationship that lasted more than three years. Six are having sex regularly with strangers and the group averages almost two partners per person per month. Three of them occasionally take part in orgies. One is a sadomasochist. One prefers boys to men. Three of the men currently are alcoholics, five have a history of alcohol abuse, and four have

a history of drug abuse. Three currently smoke cigarettes, five regularly use at least one illegal drug, and three are multiple drug users. Four have a history of acute depression, three have seriously contemplated suicide, and two have attempted suicide. Eight have a history of sexually transmitted diseases, eight currently carry infectious pathogens, and three currently suffer from digestive or urinary ailments caused by these pathogens. At least three are HIV-infected, and one has AIDS. This group is not likely to be *gay* as the older dictionaries define the term. It is estimated that the life expectancy of active homosexual males is as much as 20 years less on average than the population as a whole.

31. Jim Nelson Black, *Freefall of the American University: How our Colleges Are Corrupting the Minds and Morals of the Next Generation* (Nashville, Tenn.: Thomas Nelson, 2004) 124-5.

32. Ibid., 269.

33. Mike S. Adams, *Welcome to the Ivory Tower of Babel: Confessions of a Conservative College Professor* (Augusta, Ga.: Harbor House, 2004), Introduction.

34. Ibid., 152.

35. Ibid., 154.

36. Ibid., 156.

37. Ibid., 74.

38. Ibid., 60.

39. Ibid., 76-7.

40. Black, *Freefall of the American University*, 230.

41. Ibid., 230.

42. Ibid., 283-6.

43. Ibid., 281.

44. Ibid., 260.

45. Ibid., 265.

46. Ibid., 24.

47. Ibid., 202. Statistics cited are from "Rethinking Rites of Passage: Substance Abuse on America's Campuses: A Report by the Commission on Substance Abuse at Colleges and Universities," National Center on Addiction and Substance Abuse. June 1994.

48. Ibid., 204.

CHAPTER FOUR

1. Harriet Beecher Stowe, *Uncle Tom's Cabin*, adapted by Anne Terry White (New York: George Braziller, 1966) vii.

2. Stark, *For the Glory of God*, 342.

3. *Webster's New World College Dictionary*, 4th Edition (New York: MacMillan, 1999).

4. Ephesians 6:5-8 (RSV).

5. Stowe, *Uncle Tom's Cabin*, 416.

6. Stark, *For the Glory of God*, 291. The opening historical material in this chapter relies heavily on the historical summary in Rodney Stark's chapter on slavery, pp. 291-365.

7. Ibid., 291.

8. Ibid., 292.

9. Ibid., 299.

10. Ibid., 326.

11. Ibid., 297.

12. Ibid., 295.

13. Ibid., 338.

14. Ibid., 301, 303.

15. Ibid., 307, 318.

16. Ibid., 317-8.

17. Ibid, 304.

18. Ibid., 318.

19. Ibid., 320.

20. Ibid., 320-1.

21. Ibid., 323.

22. Ibid., 322.

23. Ibid., 291, 331.

24. Ibid., 360.

25. Matthew 22:36-38; Deuteronomy 6:5 (RSV).

26. Genesis 1:26, 27 (RSV).

27. Genesis 9:25 (RSV).

28. Leviticus 25:44 (RSV).

29. Leviticus 25:39, 42 (RSV).

30. Leviticus 25: 43, 53 (RSV).

31. Leviticus 25:10, 39-41.

32. Ephesians 6:9, (RSV). (Italics added).

33. Colossians 4:1 (RSV).

34. Acts 10: 34 (RSV).

35. Romans 2:11 (RSV).

36. Colossians 3:25 (RSV). (Italics added).

37. Galatians 3:27, 28 (RSV).

38. Colossians 3:29 (RSV).

39. Philemon v. 10 (RSV).

40. Philemon vv. 12-16 (RSV).

41. Matthew 28:19 (RSV).

42. This whole section is a very brief summary of Rodney Stark's *For the Glory of God*, pp. 338-360.

43. Ibid., 339.

44. Ibid., 340.

45. Ibid., 341.

46. Joseph J. Ellis, *Founding Brothers: The Revolutionary Generation* (New York: Knopf, 2001) 82. Article 1, Section 9 reads: "The Migration and Importation of such Persons as any of the States now existing Shall think proper to admit, Shall not be prohibited by the Congress prior to the Year one thousand eight hundred and eight."

47. Ibid., 81.

48. Ibid., 83.

49. Ibid., 89.

50. Ibid., 90.

51. Joseph J. Ellis, *His Excellency, George Washington* (New York: Knopf, 2004) 263.

52. Ellis, *Founding Brothers*, 89-90.

53. Ibid., 342.

54. Ibid., 343.

55. Ibid., 344.

56. Ibid., 350.

57. Ibid., 341.

58. Ibid., 347.

59. According to *Webster's New World College Dictionary*, "Enlightenment" was "a mainly 18th century European philosophical movement characterized by a reliance on reason and experience rather than on dogma and tradition."

60. Stark, *For the Glory of God*, 359.

61. Ibid., 359.

62. Ibid., 360.

CHAPTER FIVE

1. Rodney Stark, *The Rise of Christianity: How the Obscure, Marginal Jesus Movement Became the Dominant Religious Force in the Western World in a Few Centuries* (Princeton: Princeton University Press, 1996; San Francisco: HarperCollins paperback, 1997) 97.

2. Ibid, 97.

3. Ibid, 97-8.

4. Alan Cole, *The Epistle of Paul to the Galatians* (Grand Rapids, Mich.: Eerdmans, 1965), 111.

5. Genesis 1:27, 28 (RSV).

6. Genesis 3:16 (RSV).

7. Mark 15:41 (RSV).

8. Mark 15:47 (RSV).

9. Mark 16: 1 (RSV).

10. Mark 16:6 (RSV).

11. Luke 24:11 (RSV).

12. John 20:14-17, cf. Luke 24:1-10, Mark 16:9, Matthew 28:1-10 (RSV).

13. Matthew 22:30 (RSV).

14. Colossians 3:18, 19; Ephesians 5:21-33; I Peter 3:1-7, etc. (RSV).

15. I Peter 3:7 (RSV).

16. Ephesians 5:25 (RSV).

17. Acts 18:26 (RSV).

18. Romans 16:1 (RSV).

19. Romans 16:4 (RSV).

20. I Corinthians 11:5 (RSV).

21. I Corinthians 14:1 (RSV).

22. Philippians 4:3 (RSV).

23. Two passages that are very difficult to interpret and are not followed specifically by most churches may seem to contradict this general picture (I Corinthians 14:33-36 and I Timothy 2:9-15). They may, however, be dealing with specific local problems that are not fully explained.

24. Romans 12:4-8; I Corinthians 12:27, 28 (RSV).

25. Stark, *The Rise of Christianity*, 98.

26. Ibid., 97-8.

27. Ibid., 97.

28. Ibid., 110.

29. Winston Langley and Vivian Fox, eds., *Women's Rights in the United States: A Documentary History* (Westport, Conn.: Greenwood, 1994,) 15-6.

30. Ibid., 21.

31. Ibid., 21-2.

32. Ibid., 60-1.

33. Marsden, *The Soul of the American University*, 22.

34. Ibid., 23.

35. Langley and Fox, *Women's Rights*, 82-3.

36. Ibid., 133.

CHAPTER SIX

1. Dean E. Murray, "God, American History and a Fifth-Grade Class," *New York Times*, 5 Dec. 2004, 4Wk.

2. Glenn Tinder, *The Political Meaning of Christianity: An Interpretation* (Baton Rouge, La.: Louisiana State University Press, 1989) 7.

3. Romans 5:8 (RSV).

4. Gary DeMar, *America's Christian Heritage* (Nashville, Tenn.: Broadman and Holman, 2003).

5. Ibid., 33.

6. Quoted in Ibid, 33.

7. Ibid., 33.

8. Ibid., 33.

9. Alexis de Tocqueville, *Democracy in America*, J.P. Mayer, ed.; (New York: Anchor Books, 1969) xiv.

10. Ibid., 295.

11. Ibid., 285-6.

12. Ibid., 287-90.

13. Ibid., 288.

14. Ibid., 291.

15. Ibid., 293.

16. Peter Marshall and David Manuel, *The Light and the Glory* (New York: Revell, 1977) 73-106.

17. William Bradford, *Of Plymouth Plantation: Bradford's History of the Plymouth Settlement, 1608-1650* (San Antonio, Texas: Vision Forum, 1998).

18. Ibid., 21.

19. Ibid., 49.

20. Ibid., 77.

21. DeMar, *America's Christian Heritage*, 20-1.

22. Stated specifically in the Bill of Rights, added in 1789, in the 10th Amendment.

23. Ibid., 23.

24. Ibid., 24-5.

25. Ibid., 25.

26. Ibid., 26.

27. Ibid., 27.

28. Ibid., 27.

29. Ibid., 28.

30. Ibid., 29.

31. David Barton, *The Myth of Separation* (Aledo, Texas: Wallbuilder Press, 1992) 7.

32. Ibid., 41.

33. Ibid., 42.

34. Ibid., 42.

35. Ibid., 47-78 cf. these pages for the fuller context of each of these decisions.

36. Ibid., 48.

37. Ibid., 62.

38. Ibid., 68.

39. Ibid., 71.

40. Ibid., 77.

41. Ibid., 78.

42. Ibid., 79.

43. Ibid., 118.

44. Ibid., 123.

45. Long before *Everson*, the U.S. States Supreme Court upheld a limitation of the "free exercise" clause in *Reynolds v. United States*, a case that upheld a ban against the practice of polygamy.

46. Barton, *The Myth of Separation*, 286-7.

47. Ibid., 151.

48. Ibid., 17-8.

49. Ibid., 18.

50. Paul C. Vitz, *Censorship: Evidence of Bias in our Children's Textbooks* (Cincinnati, Ohio: Servant Books, 1986).

51. Barton, *The Myth of Separation*, 19.

52. Ibid., 19.

53. Ibid., 20.

54. Ibid., 25.

55. Tinder, *The Political Meaning of Christianity*, 27.

56. Romans 13:1-7 (RSV).

57. Mark 12:17 (RSV).

58. Romans 13:1 (RSV).

59. David Aikman, *Jesus in Beijing: How Christianity Is Transforming China and Changing the Global Balance of Power* (Washington, D.C.: Regnery, 2003) 5-6.

60. Psalms 33:12 (RSV).

CHAPTER SEVEN

1. Glenn Tinder, "Can we Be Good Without God," *Atlantic Monthly*, December 1989, later published as "A Regent College Reprint" (1993).

2. Ibid., 2.

3. Ibid., 6.

4. "In Putin's Russia Business Struggles for a Foothold," *Wall Street Journal*, 27 April 2005, A1, A8.

5. I Peter 1:13-16 (RSV).

6. I John 4:19 (RSV).

7. George Washington, "Farewell Address," quoted in William J. Bennett, ed., *Our Sacred Honor: Words of Advice from the Founders in Stories, Letters, Poems, and Speeches* (New York: Simon and Schuster, 1997) 368-9.

8. Ibid., 379-80.

9. Ibid., 367.

10. Ibid., 327.

11. Ibid., 352.

12. Ibid., 366.

13. Hadley Arkes, *Natural Rights and the Right to Choose* (Cambridge: Cambridge University Press, 2002) 1.

14. Ibid., 2.

15. Ibid., 2.

16. Ibid., 3.

17. Antonin Scalia, quoted in Mark R. Levin, *Men in Black: How the Supreme Court is Destroying America* (Washington, D.C.: Regnery, 2005) 68-69.

18. Ibid., 69.

19. Ibid., 69.

20. Robert H. Bork, "The Necessary Amendment," *First Things*, August/September 2004, 17.

21. Judges 21:25 (RSV).

22. Bork, "The Necessary Amendment," 17.

23. Matthew 22:35-40 (RSV).

24. Exodus 20: 13-17 (RSV).

25. Exodus 20: 13-17 (RSV).

26. "Church For Sale," *Lake Champlain Weekly*, 16 March 2005, 5.

27. Barbara Dafoe Whitehead and David Popenoe, "The State of Our Unions," *Theology Matters*, March/April 2004, 1-7. The statistics in this section, in the main, are taken from this article.

28. Maggie Gallagher, "What Marriage Is For," *Theology Matters*, March/April 2004, 10.

29. Ibid., 11.

30. Ibid., 10.

31. Gene Edward Veith, "The Nordic Track," *Theology Matters*, March/April 2004, 14.

32. Ibid., 14.

33. Ibid., 14.

34. Ibid., 15.

35. Hadley Arkes, "Bush's Second Chance," *First Things*, April 2005, 14.

36. Ibid., 15.

37. Ibid., 16.

38. Arkes, *Natural Rights and the Right to Choose*, 109-10.

39. Ibid., 126-7.

40. For a fuller treatment of this theme, cf. Ibid., Ch. 5.

41. Arkes, "Bush's Second Chance," 18.

42. From the description of Dr. Martin Haskell, one of the inventors of the partial-birth abortion procedure, as quoted in Arkes, *Natural Rights and the Right to Choose*, 103.

43. James 1:27 (KJV).

44. Stark, *The Rise of Christianity*, 119.

45. Ibid., 121.

46. Ibid., 125.

47. Matthew 11:28, 29 (RSV).

CHAPTER EIGHT

1. Harris, *The End of Faith*, 11-2.

2. Ibid., 12-4.

3. Stark, *For the Glory of God*, 49.

4. Quoted in Stark, *One True God* (Princeton, N.J.: Princeton University Press, 2001) 136.

5. Ibid., 135-7.

6. Stark, *For the Glory of God*, 50-1.

7. Ibid., 48.

8. Ibid., 48-9.

9. Ibid., 48.

10. Stark, *The Rise of Christianity*, 49.

11. Quoted in Stark, *One True God*, 125.

12. Stark, *For the Glory of God*, 48.

13. I John 5:4 (RSV).

14. Stark, *For the Glory of God*, 203, 215. For an entire chapter on the subject, see Chapter 3.

15. Ibid., 224.

16. Ibid., 224.

17. Ibid., 226.

18. Ibid., 278-9.

19. Ibid., 285-6.

20. Ibid., 256.

21. Ibid., 257.

CHAPTER NINE

1. An ancient anonymous Hindu poem.

2. Harris, *The End of Faith*, 15.

3. Alan Dershowitz, quoted on the jacket of *The End of Faith*.

4. John 3:16 (RSV).

5. Here is a sampling of passages:

Matthew 11:28	Matthew 26:26-28	Mark 10:45
Luke 15:11-24	John 1:12	John 3:16-18
John 11:25	Acts 2:38	Acts 16:30, 31
Romans 3:23-25	Romans 5:1	Romans 6:23
I Corinthians 15:1-5	II Corinthians 5:14-21	Galatians 1:15, 16
Ephesians 2:8-10	Philippians 3:1-9	Colossians 3:13, 14
I Timothy 3:16	II Timothy 1:8-10	Titus 1:11-14
Hebrews 12:1, 2	I Peter 1:3-9	I John 1-9
I John 4:9, 10	Revelation 3:20.	

6. Luke in Acts 4:42 says that the early Christians "devoted themselves to the Apostles teaching [the Bible] and fellowship [the family of Christians], to the breaking of bread [worship] and the prayers [conversations with God in prayer]" (RSV).

7. Romans 15:13 (RSV).

ABOUT THE AUTHOR

The Rev. Russ Stevenson, presently the organizing pastor of a new church development in Gonzales, Louisiana, served as pastor of First Presbyterian Church in Baton Rouge for 20 years, a church of 1,600 members, the largest Presbyterian church in the state.

An honors graduate of Princeton University (A.B.), he received a B.D. from Fuller Theological Seminary and a Th.M. from Princeton Seminary.

Rev. Stevenson has an active writing ministry, contributing columns and articles to newspapers and Presbyterian publications.

He and his wife, Sherrill, have four daughters and 21 grandchildren.

LaVergne, TN USA
21 April 2010
179942LV00001B/42/P